EXEGETICAL STUDY OF ANGELS & DEMONS

Exegetical Study of Angels & Demons

David Vincent Williams

January, 2017

Xulon Elite

Xulon Press Elite
2301 Lucien Way #415
Maitland, FL 32751
407.339.4217
www.xulonpress.com

Exulon
Elite

© 2017 by David Vincent Williams

All rights reserved solely by the author. The author guarantees all contents are original and do not infringe upon the legal rights of any other person or work. No part of this book may be reproduced in any form without the permission of the author. The views expressed in this book are not necessarily those of the publisher.

Scripture quotations taken from The Original African Heritage Bible, King James Version (KJV)–*public domain.*

Printed in the United States of America.

ISBN-13: 9781498498302

ACKNOWLEDGMENTS

I would like to take this opportunity to thank my wife, and my mother that transitioned in 2011, for their encouragement to further my studies at the Doctoral level. With their support and my spiritual faith in God, made this opportunity an enlightening endeavor of study and research.

CONTENTS

ACKNOWLEDGMENTS VII
INTRODUCTION XI

PART 1

CHERUBIM 3
RANKS OF ANGELS 9
ANGELOLOGY 13
ANGELS IN THE NEW AND OLD TESTAMENTS 16
ANGELIC ENCOUNTERS IN OUR DAILY LIVES 22

PART 2

STORY OF AN ANGEL 35
RELATIONSHIP BETWEEN GOD - ANGELS
    AND HUMANS 40
ANGELS AND CHILDREN 45
SATAN 50

PART 3

DEMONS..61
ETHICAL AND MORAL DIVISION AGAINST GOD........67
SATANISM 71
CLOSE ANALYSIS OF SATAN AND HIS DEMONS 75

PART 4

CONTROVERSY: HELL; DOES IT EXIST?............. 83
SATAN'S EVIL INTENTIONS?....................... 89
MENTAL ILLNESS 97
HOMOSEXUALITY.................................101
BRIEF ANALYSIS: THE ENEMY 107
CLOSING REMARKS 111

INTRODUCTION

We will look into this vivid and vast world that human beings share together, as well as an intrigued measure evolving around the behaviors of the angelic and demonic worlds, and what they have to offer in concurrence with our lives and that of our Lord God and Savior Jesus Christ(Yeshua).

Many children that were born and raised in the United States were often told stories about angels, and how they are spiritual beings that are in the heavens, that are sent by God to protect, and watch over us. Considering when a loved one dies, we share information that God will give the deceased individual a pair of wings in heaven, to be with our Lord and Savior, to further God's mission of love towards the human race.

In 1986, Billy Graham stated that there is evidence from scripture as well as one's personal life, that individual guardian angels, hover over our lives and protect us.[1]

---

[1] Draper, Scott, and Joseph O. Baker. "Angelic Belief as American Folk Religion." *Sociological Forum* 26, no. 3 (September 2011): 623-643.

Truly; one must ask themselves, what are angels, and are they good for humanity, and what are their specific duties? Many have suggested that Satan the devil, and his demons (lower angels in rank to Satan), were kicked out of heaven, and here on earth to wreak havoc because Satan believes he's superior to God. Is this myth, or false religious doctrine? What are some of the things in life we often wrestle with in today's society? These are just some of the inquiries that will be researched, analyzed and answered.

Many of our church leaders and every human being on earth should be aware that angels and demons exist, and are a part of our human and spiritual lives.

This book will address angels and demons in contrast of their light and darkness, and if they have any emotions and or feelings, and involve themselves in worldly affairs.

Everything you always wanted to know about angels and demons will are addressed. My conclusions and concepts about angels and demons are based on Biblical and scholarly research; that will are used for the foundation and analysis of this book. All facts are based on research pros and cons.

I truly hope that this book will enlighten and inspire. May the Holy Spirit guide me in obtaining true and concise research that will ultimately develop a better understanding of Angelology and Demonology as it pertains to our current lives as we share this earth with one another.

PART 1

CHERUBIM / CHERUB

In the Lost Books of the Bible or any other Bible, e.g. NIV or King James, we are certain to read about the creation story of Adam and Eve and the first encounter they had with the serpent(Satan) in the Garden of Eden, in the book of Genesis.

Irving H. Skolnick, suggests that the first encounter with angels occurred when Adam and Eve banished from the Garden of Eden and met by *cherubim* at the east of the garden.[2]

Satan and his serpents attempt were to destroy God's conception, by tempting Eve with eating a forbidden fruit from the tree of knowledge, that God instructed Adam and Eve not to eat.

As a result, when Satan tempted Eve, and thus advised Adam to eat from the tree of knowledge – is when God told the both of them to depart from the Garden of Eden. As they both walked from the Garden of Eden, Adam saw a *cherub* swinging a sword that

---

[2] Skolnick, Irving H. *"THE HIDDEN MISSION OF BIBLICAL ANGELS."* Jewish Bible Quarterly 38, no. 1 2010

contained the fire, as the cherub frowned at the both of them[3] That scared Adam and Eve, and the both of them fell on their faces.[4]

Since the *cherub* or *cherubim* are the first obedient angel(s) mentioned in the Bible, let's take a moment to discuss the *cherub* angel.

One might ask; what are the duties of a *cherub*? In the book of Genesis, the *cherubim* are described as the guard(s) at the gate of the Garden of Eden, and thus had a ferocious like appearance, according to McLeod.[5]

According to William Albright, "the primary function of the *cherub* in Israelite religious symbolism is illustrated by two Biblical passages. A very ancient hymn, found twice in the Bible, has the words, "And he rode upon a cherub and did fly" (1 Sam 22:11, Ps. 18:11); the second passage is Ezek. 10:20. [6]

Bethany House Publishers suggests that angels were mistaken for men (humans), and have frightened the people that have come into contact with them.[7]

---

[3] Joseph B. Lumpkin, "Lost Books of the Bible" p. 13

[4] Joseph B. Lumpkin, "Lost Books of the Bible" p. 13

[5] Cherubim and Cherub are thus described as the angel that guards the Garden of Eden. Frank E. McLeod, "Angels Q&A" p. 9.

[6] lbright, William Foxwell. "*What were the cherubim?*" Biblical Archaeologist 1, no. 1 (February 1938): 1-3. ATLA Religion Database with ATLASerials

[7] Bethany House Publishers. *Everything the Bible says about Angels and Demons*, p. 7

Cherubim / Cherub

Theodorus, the Bishop of Heraclea, says that the *Cherubim* does not have any angelic powers, and is a horrible beast which scared Adam from the entrance of the Garden of Eden (paradise).[8]

Also, Philo concludes that the cherubim(s) are the first angels mentioned in the Old Testament, in the book of (Genesis 3:22).

There are two *cherubim's* are mentioned in the book of Exodus(25:18) that are on both sides of the Ark of the Covenant. The *Cherubim* symbolizes God's "highest and most chief potencies, sovereignty, and goodness." [9]

We can very well conclude that in quintessence, that the very first angel that was mentioned in the Bible was an angel of darkness (Satan).

Satan tempted Eve, and as a result, both Adam and Eve were dismissed from paradise-(Garden of Eden). Satan; (seraphim in rank) was the supreme angel in the choir of the *Cherubim* angels[10]

According to the Muslim lore, the *cherubim* was a creation of the tears of Michael over sins of the faithful. In the Canaanite; the people who were the original Israelites were familiar with the cherubim from the Genesis accounts, as well as accounts in the Old Testament. They would call the cherubim, "winged beast with human heads." [11]

---

[8] Gustav Davidson. "A Dictionary of Angels including the fallen angels." p.86.

[9] Gustav Davidson, 1967, p. 86

[10] Davidson, p.86.

[11] Davidson, p.87.

As children growing up in the United States, one would always see paintings as well as pictures of God sitting on cherubim.

Also, the God of Israel was labeled as "He who sitteth on the *cherubim* (1 Sam 4:4).[12]

The book of Enoch is considered to have a vast array of specifics on angels, especially the *cherubim (cherub)* on the occasion(s) of the Garden of Eden by God's instruction.

The book of Enoch described the cherub as being angry and frowned at them, and as a result, both Adam and Eve fell to their faces, because they were afraid and thought that the *Cherub* would do them harm. "But he had pity on them and showed them mercy." [13]

The cherub then went up to heaven and thus, prayed to God and said, "Lord you sent me to watch at the gate of the garden with a sword of fire. But when your servants, Adam, and Eve, saw me, they fell on their faces and were as dead. Oh my Lord, what shall we do to your servants? Then God had pity on them, and showed them mercy, and sent his angel to keep the garden." [14]

There are a few things in chapter three that the *cherub* does that are in question. First, the cherub is described as being angry, and then he shows mercy, and then prayed to the Lord. Do angels

---

[12] Albright, William Foxwell. *"What were the cherubim?"* Biblical Archaeologist 1, no. 1

[13] Chapter 3 vs 10, 11. Lumpkin, Joseph B. *Lost Books of the Bible: The Great Rejected Text.*

[14] Chapter 3 vs 11-14. Lumpkin, Joseph B. *Lost Books of the Bible: The Great Rejected Text.*

have feelings? According to chapter three in the book of Enoch, I would say, yes.

However, there are several ranks of angels, and each rank has a specific duty or task. As we can clearly note; the cherub is an angel that is compassionate, and follows the command(s) of our Lord God.

Conclusion

We have stated that the lost books of the Bible contain evidence that there was a serpent in the book of Genesis that tempted Eve in Garden of Eden that subsequently involved Adam, and was perhaps the first encounter with an angel (serpent).

From this, we know that when Adam and Eve banished from the Garden – they were met by a *Cherub/Cherubim* – an angel of God.

The *Cherub* is the first compliant angel that is mentioned in the Bible. Genesis 3:22, confirms this, and confirmed by Philo, a philosopher from Alexandria Egypt – born in 25 BC, who was taught by Socrates who were both taught by the Egyptians, according to Herodotus, the Greek historian.

Ultimately, the *cherub's* duties are to guard the entrance of the Garden of Eden, and according to Frank McLeod – the *cherub* has a fierce appearance and do not have angelic powers, but scared Adam from the entrance of the Garden of Eden – according to Theodorus, the Bishop of Heraclea.

In Muslim lore accounts the *cherubim's* were conceived by the tears of Michael over the sins of the truthful.

The original Canaanite Israelites were very familiar with the accounts of the cherubim in the Old Testament, and the Genesis accounts and would refer to the *cherubim* as the winged beast with human heads, as well as the book of Enoch, that has accounts of the *cherubim* as well.

RANKS OF ANGELS

*B*ethany House Publishers provides a brief explanation on Angels: "Angels are active spirits" - observed John Wesley. They ascend to give an account of what they have done and to receive orders and descend to execute the orders they have received.

In John 1:51, Jesus says he is the ladder by which there is an interaction between heaven and earth." [15]

Thomas Aquinas (Summa Theologica 1.108) suggests that the cherubim is ranked in the hierarchies in the following order:

1. Seraphim, Cherubim, and Thrones.

According to Kreeft; The *Seraphim* is the highest choir that understand God with the highest precision, and thus their love is considered to be the hottest. Seraphim also means "Light – bearer" and Satan was one of them and the reasons for Satan being commanding as well as hazardous.

---

[15] Bethany House Publishers. *Everything the Bible says about Angels and Demons*, p.19.

The *Cherubim*; according to Kreeft, means fullness of wisdom. They also anticipate God as well.

Thrones, symbolize judicial power and also contemplate God.

2. Dominations, Virtues, and Powers

Dominations mean authority, and they command the lesser angels that are below them, according to Kreeft.

Virtues receive orders from dominations and run the universe in especially heavenly realms.

Powers serve the virtues by fighting evil.

3. Principalities, Archangels, and Angels[16]

Principalities are the angels that care for cities, nations as well as kingdoms.

Archangels such as (Gabriel and Michael), carry God's important messages to man. *Angels* are our guardian angels, and there is one angel for each on earth.

The above-referenced[17] material can be attributed to Peter Kreeft.

It is appropriate to mention *Dion the Areopagite*. Dion the Areopagite was a judge who was mentioned in the Acts of the

---

[16] Dionysius the Areopagite. "The Celestial Hierarchy" introduction.

[17] Kreeft, Peter. *Angels and Demons, What do we really know about them?* P. 75.

Apostles (Acts 17:34). He was also a convert to Christianity by the evangelizations of the Apostle Paul. [18]

It is, therefore, probable to include the following from Dion the Areopagite since it is thus, works of Angelology:

> "It is, therefore, lawful to portray Beings in forms drawn from even the lowest of material things which are not discordant since they, too, having originated from that which is truly beautiful, have throughout the whole of their bodily constitution some vestiges of intellect and beauty, and through these we may be led to immaterial Archetypes; the similitudes being taken, as has been said, dissimilarity, and the same things being defined, not in the same way, but harmoniously and fittingly, in the case both of intellectual and sensible natures."[19]

Conclusion

We have concluded that angels are active spirits that report back to God regarding what they have done, and receive their orders from God and to follow through with the orders they have received

---

[18] Kreeft, Peter. *Angels and Demons, What do we really know about them?* P. 75
Dionysius the Areopagite. "The Celestial Hierarchy" introduction..

[19] Dionysius the Areopagite. "The Celestial Hierarchy" p. 18

from God. Jesus is the bridge by which there are the interactions between the heavens and the earth.

Also – we have discussed the different ranks such as the Seraphim – being the highest angel regarding rank, means "light bearer." We have discovered that Satan was in the order of one of the highest ranks of angels, but as we well know – rebelled against God and became very dangerous.

Dion the Areopagite, who was a judge and convert to Christianity, suggest the no matter the rank of angels, they are beautiful and intellectual beings in nature.

ANGELOLOGY

Angelology is the study of angels, and the study of the nature of God, as well as Theology.

In fact – Landes suggests that Angelology, as well as Theology, is related in that the survey of the Old Testament demonstrates the certainty of this.[20]

Angels are also referred to as "host," and are also referred to as the "sons of God" because of their relationship with God. Angels are the unbegotten sons of God while Jesus is referred to as the only begotten son of God. [21]

We touched a bit on Dionysius, and is important to note that the *Celestial Hierarchy* was an important text on angelology, written by Angelology reached its peak in the thirteenth century

---

[20] Landes, George M. "Shall we neglect the angels." *Union Seminary Quarterly Review* 14, no. 4 (May 1959): 19-25. *ATLA Religion Database with ATLASerials*, EBSCO*host*, p.21.

[21] Phillips, Ron. *Angels and Demons*. {Lake Mary, Florida: Charisma House, 2015}.

According to Merriam-Webster dictionary, Angelology is defined as the theological doctrine of angels or its study. [22]

Merriam-Webster defines Demonology as a study of demons and evil spirits.[23] We will thus begin our study of angelology and demonology, beginning with angelology, and ending this paper with demonology.

According to Giorgio Agamben; Thomas Aquinas and Pseudo – Dionysius, are the church fathers on Angelology and find their appropriate place in the administration of this world, and anything that suggests that angelology should be separated from governmental vocation – is doomed to failure.[24]

Agamben also suggests that the Talmud, which is the Jewish law from the elders -suggest that in the time of trouble, Michael and Gabriel are not the ones that one should cry too, but should cry to Christ.

---

[22] "Angelology." Merriam-Webster.com. Accessed September 30, 2015. http://www.merriam-webster.com/dictionary/angelology.

[23] Demonology." *Merriam-Webster.com*. Merriam-Webster, n.d. Web. 30 Sept. 2015. <http://www.merriam-webster.com/dictionary/demonology>. : belief in demons : a doctrine of evil spirits

[24] gamben, Giorgio. "*ANGELS*." Angelaki: Journal of the Theoretical Humanities 16, no. 3

Conclusion

The theological doctrine that is primarily related to Theology and the survey of the Old Testament – according to Giorgio Agamben, Thomas Aquinas, and Pseudo – Dionysius, were the church fathers on Angelology.

Angelology is needed because of the relationship Angels have with God, and is that pertinent information that should be studied, for us to see the love and the relationship that God seeks to have with his creation (us).

We must also be forever reminded, that although angels do good things for us in times of desperate need(s), we should not seek the angels for assistance but always seek God first.

ANGELS IN THE NEW & OLD TESTAMENT

―――――⁕―――――

Angels play a significant role in being messengers in the New Testament. The following accounts can be attributed to Frank E. McLeod. [25] For one, we can recall the angel Gabriel that God sent to deliver a message to Mary – which she was chosen to birth the Messiah.

Another account – is when an angel appeared to Joseph in a dream and advised him that God has chosen his wife to bear his child – the Messiah.

Also, another notable account of angels – is when they appeared to the shepherds, and after the birth of Jesus is when the angels of the Lord appeared to Joseph, advising him to take Mary and the baby Jesus into Egypt, to avoid the advances of King Herod.

"And when they were departed, behold, the angel of the Lord appeareth to Joseph in a dream, saying, Arise, and take the young

---

[25] McLeod, Frank E. *Angels Q&A*. {Frank E. McLeod, 2013}, 55.

child and mother, and flee into Egypt, and be there until I bring thee word: for Herod will seek the young child to destroy him." [26]

According to McLeod, there are no more accounts of angels until Matthew 3 and 4, with the baptism of Christ as well as when Satan tried to tempt Jesus, and afterward, angels came and ministered unto him in Matthew 4:11.

After this, we do not see any mentioning of angels in Jesus's ministry but mentions angels regarding his return to earth.[27]

Another notable occurrence of angels is when they appeared to Jesus in the garden of Gethsemane, These accounts were so severe, that Jesus was sweating drops of blood, and an angel appeared to Jesus strengthening him (Luke 22:43).

The next occurrence with angels occurred in the resurrection of Jesus in Matthew 28:1-6, and Luke 24:4-5 – but the accounts do not mention angels but mention two men in shining garments.[28]

McLeod suggests that in the second coming, angels are heavily involved and can be searched through the following passages.

Matthew. 13:39

Matthew. 13:31

Matthew. 13:49

Matthew. 16:27

---

[26] McLeod, Frank E. *Angels Q&A*. {Frank E. McLeod, 2013}, p.57.

[27] McLeod, Frank E. *Angels Q&A*. {Frank E. McLeod, 2013},p. 57,58

[28] McLeod, Frank E. *Angels Q&A*. {Frank E. McLeod, 2013}, p 58, 59.

Matthew. 25:31

Matthew. 8:38

Lastly, McLeod explains that the book of revelation has accounts of angels in the following passages.

Rev. 8:7

Rev. 8:8

Rev.8:10

Rev. 8:12

Rev. 9:1

Rev.9:13

Rev. 11:15.

Rev. 21:9

Rev. 22:16

Let us examine Matthew 4:11. Matthew was a tax collector and disciple of Jesus Christ. The book of Matthew was mainly written to a Jewish audience that had promises of the Messiah – the one that the Jews had anticipated for many years [29]

Matthew 4: 11- suggest that Jesus had received strength from the angels after Satan's attempt to wear Jesus out through a series of test. Satan failed miserably and left Jesus. Then the angels appeared to give Jesus power – to carry on with his mission.

---

[29] Kent, Paul. *"Knowing your Bible."* Barbour publishing 2013.

Also, Luke chapter 4 – is about the testing of Jesus in the wilderness and the accounts that the book of Luke chapter 4, is very similar to the book of Matthew, regarding angel activity.

In the Old Testament, in regards to the book of 1Kings 19:6-8, suggest that Elijah had received food from an angel once he became tired and depressed from battling false prophets and spiritual warfare. Elijah wanted to end his life until an angel appeared and baked him bread and a jar of water to regain his strength.

"Angels strengthen on serious assignment from God. Angels do not strengthen one simply because he or she is tired; they are available to those on kingdom assignments." [30]

"The angel of the Lord came back a second time, and touched him and said, "Get up and eat, for the journey is too much for you." So he got up and ate and drank the food and traveled for forty days and forty nights until he reached Horeb, the mountain of God. From there he went into a cave, where he spent the night.[31]

The last Old Testament occurrence with angelic activity occurs in Daniel 10:17, 18. This chapter is unique, because Daniel was very faithful to God, and thus was a blessed man. His angelic experience consisted of someone looking like a man that gave him strength after telling Daniel not to be afraid and that he was highly favored.

---

[30] Phillips, Ron. *Our Invisible Allies*. {Lake Mary, Florida: Charisma House, 2009}.

[31] NIV Study Bible. Zondervan, 1973.

We can affirm that Angels play a significant roles in human life dating back to the Old and New Testaments, and I am sure that angels will continue to be a part of the human experience in our future.

Michael Welker suggests that "when God becomes present in angels, it amounts to God's relative finalization of self.[32]

We all have at one time or another - have experienced an angel's presence at least once in our lives. In the next chapter we will look into some of the angel stories we encounter, whether we experienced it ourselves, or hearing it from someone else.

Conclusion

Angels play a significant role as messengers in the New Testament. For instance, when an Angel appeared to Joseph in a dream, Gabriel, was sent to deliver a message to Mary regarding her being selected (by God) to birth the Messiah.

There are more angelic instances, when Satan tried to tempt Jesus, when an angel appeared to Jesus in the garden of Gethsemane to strengthen him.

The appearance of angels in the New Testament is proof that angels follow the direction of God for reasons that purify our hearts to bring us closer to him. The accounts in this section prove that we serve a loving God and that he only wants us to succeed.

---

[32] Welker, Michael. *"Angels in the biblical traditions."* Theology Today 51, no. 3, p. 370.

The angels are sent as a reminder that God is always watching and sending his angels to direct his grace in a loving manner and giving us the strength we need, at the exact time we need it.

ANGELIC ENCOUNTERS IN OUR DAILY LIVES

We often hear of someone saying that they had an encounter with an angel, and sometimes their stories can sound quite convincing. However, according to Boa and Bowman, [33] there are instances perhaps where that person was either mistaking a human being to be an angel or either that person is lying.

Encounters with angels during Biblical times were very rare occasions and did exist, and are ever so active, but are always invisible to the human eye.

However, it is wise to suggest, that in most cases, there is not enough information, and thus we should conclude that we just don't know.[34]

---

[33] Boa, Kenneth D & Bowman, Robert M Jr. *Sense & Nonsense about Angels & Demons.* {Zondervan, 2007}p. 96

[34] Boa & Bowman, 2007, p.97

We must also recognize that angels whose messages that do not conform to scripture are concluded as either demonic and or imagined, according to Gal 1:8, 2 Cor 11: 4, Tim 4: 1, and 1 John 4:1. [35]

Also, those angels that introduce new doctrine and or new practices into what is already, in Christianity, are not from God.

Thus, we should conclude that if a *non-believer* is comforted by an angel, it is not from God and anyone who says that he or she has had conversations with angels, even though scripture is quoted word for word, remain cautious.

All angels were created perfect, and so was Lucifer. He was one of the top angels in the ranks of angels. When he rebelled from God and was tossed out of heaven, he took with him, some angels that had less rank than him, and were considered as his helpers (demons) were also in opposition to God and his people [36]

Angels also have wills, emotions and have great intelligence. They are also the protectors of God. [37]

---

[35] Boa & Bowman, 2007, p.99

[36] Dickason, C. Fred. *Angels – Elect &Evil*. {Moody Publishers, 1975}, p. 170.

[37] Dickason, C. Fred. *Angels – Elect &Evil*. {Moody Publishers, 1975}, p 34-35, & 66.

According to Ron Phillips, angels were brought to life by God and given a timeless existence very different from that of a human existence[38]

Later in this paper, we will discuss research to the observance of Satan and his demons, so that we can fully understand how Satan and his demons operate.

While it is always a good thing to know about the good things that angels contribute towards the betterment of the human society, it is also good to know the downside of those angels that do not do well for humanity, but their dedication is predicated on the destruction of humanity instead.

> "Angels belong to the class of spirit beings, that is, they are understood as immaterial incorporeal beings. They certainly do not have a material, a fleshly body such as humans.
> (1) Angels are described in Hebrews 1:4 as all ministering spirits.
> (2) demons, if assumed to be fallen angels, are called evil spirits (Lk 8:2).
> (3). Evil spirits (Lk 8:2) and unclean spirits (Lk 11: 24, 26)."[39]

We can only accept that good angel, as well as bad angels, adopt a sense of knowledge from the goodness and love that God has

---

[38] Phillips, Ron. *Angels and Demons*. {Lake Mary, Florida: Charisma House, 2015}, p 15.

[39] Dickason, C. Fred. *Angels – Elect & Evil*. {Moody Publishers, 1975}, p. 33.

shown towards his creation. In that same token, bad angels seeing and knowing the goodness of the Lord can only seek to destroy.

We have seen a vast majority of the world swayed away from Christian values. The world has become so obsessed with money and status, that we forget that the goodness of God the Father, who provides and not forgetting those who partake into the equation of "those that have plenty" but do not share with others.

Good angels will do everything in their power to help us in terms of making right decisions, which will put a smile on the face of God, because God wants us to make good decisions and love one another. Angels want what is good for us too. It's their job.

During Biblical times, God would send a messenger (angel) to guide us towards the direction that is more likely to have a positive outcome. Angels, in general, are called the sons of God.[40]

In the Old Testament, the angel of God acts as the messenger of God from Abraham to the time of Zechariah, and his title was the name of *Elohim* (the mighty one).[41]

Research suggests that angels do good things for the human race, and they too have feelings for us, as illustrated when Adam was tossed out of the Garden of Eden, and how the (cherub) felt sorry for both Adam and Eve.

It is important to understand that "The ministry of angels to God, Christ, and believers is wide and varied. They are primarily

---

[40] Dickason, C. Fred. *Angels – Elect &Evil*. {Moody Publishers, 1975}, p.79.

[41] Dickason, C. Fred. *Angels – Elect &Evil*. {Moody Publishers, 1975}, p. 78

Exegetical Study of Angels & Demons

servants and messengers of God to accomplish his purpose. Scripture makes it clear that God is in no way dependent upon his subservient creatures (Job 4:18; 15:15).[42]

Although we are to respect and may admire angels, we are not to worship them or give them undue attention. They, too, are servants of Christ." [43]

According to Eileen Freeman, who is a publisher of a magazine called Angel Watch, each one of us has a guardian angel that are wise and loving – that offer help whether we ask for it or not, but the majority of us ignore them.[44]

Jews Christians and Muslims have universal ideas when it comes to angels and the roles they play in our lives. All three religions claim that angels exist. Buddhism, Hinduism, and Zoroastrianism, also believe in angels as well.

Roman Catholic theologians are more dogmatic than Biblical when it comes to angels. Protestant theologians with exclusions have ignored the angelic sensations altogether.[45]

---

[42] Dickason, C. Fred. *Angels – Elect & Evil.* {Moody Publishers, 1975}, p. 100,101.

[43] Dickason, C. Fred. *Angels – Elect & Evil.* {Moody Publishers, 1975}, p. 111.

[44] Gibbs, Nancy, and Sam Allis. "Angels among us. (Cover story)." *Time* 142, no. 27 (December 27, 1993): 56. *MAS Ultra - School Edition.*

[45] Landes, George M. "Shall we neglect the angels." *Union Seminary Quarterly Review* 14, no. 4 (May 1959): 19-25. *ATLA Religion Database with ATLASerials*, EBSCO*host*, p.19.

Protestants have little use for angels because they feel that there is a void when it comes to the relationship between man and God, and angels in some manner interfere with the direct relationship between man and God. Medieval theologians believed that the angels are the ones that fill in the gaps between God and humanity (Gibbs & Allis, 1993).

Regarding the Hebrew authors of the Bible, there were not any specific duties or obligations that the Israelite believer had to conform too when it came to angels, nor did it constitute any additional religious practices for the believer as well.[46]

Also, to answer a question that was addressed at the beginning of this paper in the introduction, regarding a deceased person(s) earning wings after death. The following statement is addressed as follow.

Reverend John Westerhoff – a pastoral theologian at Duke University School of Divinity, suggests that humans do not become angels because there is no evidence in classical theology that suggest same (Gibbs & Allis, 1993).

Westerhoff also suggests why some people can see angels while others cannot. It all stems from one's faith, and that Angels exist through the eyes of faith, and faith is perception, and for some, their faith does not have room for angels (Gibbs & Allis, 1993).

---

[46] Landes, George M. "Shall we neglect the angels." *Union Seminary Quarterly Review* 14, no. 4 (May 1959): 19-25. *ATLA Religion Database with ATLASerials*, EBSCO*host*, P.20.

However, Fifty percent of adult Americans believe in angels, according to a Gallup poll taken back in 1988.[47]

I would like to share J.P. Moreland's testimony regarding his angel experience.

JP Moreland, who is a theologian, philosopher, Apologist, and the author of many books on subjects that he has studied. JP Moreland, has said to have had an angel experience, but has never seen any angels, but are certain that angels exist. Moreland explains that he was attending church when a woman addressed him by saying that while he was talking, there were three angels that were standing beside him.

As the weeks progressed, Dr. Moreland had been experiencing a tremendous amount regarding grief. He and prayed to God, asking God, if the angels that the lady experienced seeing around him was real, and if (God) could send them (the angels) to him because at that time he felt over stricken with grief. He needed help with his grief, and then he went to sleep, after praying his prayer request.

Afterward, one of Dr. Moreland's students sent him an email, and told Dr. Moreland, that while he was teaching a class, there were three angels that were around him, and the student drew a picture of what he saw. Dr. Moreland took a look at the picture and said to himself, the three angels in the drawing that the student drew, was exactly in the same position that the lady had earlier described earlier.[48]

---

[47] Woodward, Kenneth L., and Anne Underwood. "Angels." *Newsweek* 122, no. 26 (December 27, 1993): 52. *Academic Search Premier*, EBSCO*host*

[48] Moreland, J.P. information was accessed from www.jpmoreland.com

Dr. Moreland goes on and states that angels and demons do exist, and even though he has not visibly seen angels nor demons, he suggests that he has credible friends that have credible credentials, such as Ph.D.'s, that have seen angels and have had demonic experiences and that they are credible and sane people.

Earlier, I had stated that I feel reluctant to discuss angelic experiences, because, for one, the experiences that I have experienced was when I was young, and at an age where my mother would put me to bed, in her room where I took a nap.

Conclusion

We have concluded that sometimes we may run into people that are either lying regarding when-when it comes to reports of angels. We have also concluded in biblical times, angels were present, but rarely, according to Boa and Bowman. We must also acknowledge when there is not enough evidence, we must concede that we don't know. However, I will conclude that angels do exist, and are here as our protectors. I often ask the angels after asking God to protect me in certain instances. To know that your guardian angel is protecting you, you must first form a personal relationship with God. We talk to God and cannot see Him, but conclusions tell us that he (God) and his son are with us as well.

Unbelievers are more subjective to being approached by an angel of darkness rather than an angel of light, and those angels that produce new doctrine, new scripture, and practices – are more likely to be an angel of darkness (Satan).

Today on social media, I am finding that more people come to the conclusion, that there is no Jesus, and that Jesus was a made up fairy tale because of the inscriptions on the walls that the Egyptians created and can be seen today as proof.

Egypt and its coherts are mentioned in the Bible over 700 times, and Ethiopia is mentioned in the Bible over 40 times, tells me that Christianity was a big part of Egypt as well as Ethiopia. Both countries are located in Africa. In addition, many of the Biblical prophets to include Moses and Paul, were mistaken for Egyptians (Acts 21:38) and (Exodus 2:19). [49][50]

So, I say all of this to say that Satan is confusing people and giving them false doctrines by suggesting that Christ does not exist because they believe in Egyptian deities. Egyptian writings existed many years before the birth of Christ and because of this, many are subjected to believe in African Egyptian deities than in Jesus Christ.

Angels were created perfect, and so was Satan. They also have emotions and feelings, and great intelligence. They were also brought to life by God and given a timeless life – different from human life. Angels do not have fleshly bodies like humans and are classified by their rank. There are good and bad angels. The good

---

[49] Windsor, Rudolph R. *"From Babylon to Timbuktu"* Windsor Golden Series, 2003.

[50] Felder, Cain Hope. *The Original African Heritage Study Bible* (King James Version). {Judson Press, 2007}.

angels conform to the teachings of the Lord while the bad angels and just the opposite and seek to destroy human life and the relationship that we have with the Lord.

The sons of God during biblical times were those angels sent by God that are more likely to have positive results once the angel has delivered the message from God. Those angels do good things for the human race, but God is NOT dependent on angels, and also, we are high-ranking over all angels as believers in Christ, which gives one the indication of the love that God has towards his creation.

Most of us are blind and ignore the fact that angels are here to help us, and we often ignore any advice or help offered to us by way of angels.

Again (In conclusion), all three religions – Judaism, Christianity, and Islam, do believe in the angelic realm.

Hinduism, Buddhism, and Zoroastrianism believe in angels as well. Protestants, on the other hand, do not have any use for angels and feel that they create and broken link between man and God.

We have also considered that when we die, we do not earn a pair of wings and turn into angels because there is no evidence of such occurrences in Scripture.

PART 2

STORY OF AN ANGEL

Many people are reluctant to discuss encounters with angels, but in the past, I've had personally experienced a case where someone appeared at the same location that was not there before and gave me sound advice during a critical moment. That advice changed the atmosphere – as if there were calm and peace surrounding us at the time of the intervention, which brings up an interesting question – whether angels work through people?

It is only appropriate to share a story about an encounter that a woman by the name of Ann Canady that had her own personal encounter with an angel.

Ann is married to her husband Gary, who is an Air Force retired Master Sargent. In July 1977 (coincidentally – the same month and year I joined the military) is when Ann found out that she had advanced uterine cancer. Gary, Ann's husband, lost his first wife from the same disease and was not sure if he had the strength to go through the pain with Ann. They both spend countless time praying. Ann wanted to die quickly and did not want Gary to go through this again with her. Again, Gary had already been through this with his first wife.

One morning, three days before she was going to admit herself to the hospital for surgery, the doorbell rang, and standing at the door was a large tall man. According to Ann – "He was the blackest black I've ever seen, and his eyes were a deep – deep – azure blue."

He introduced himself as Thomas and told Ann that her cancer was gone. Both Ann and Gary were puzzled and wondered how the man (Thomas) knew her name. They asked him to come inside their home and told them to stop worrying and then quoted scripture to them – Isaiah 53:5 "… and with his stripes, we are healed." Ann still looking confused and asked Thomas – demanding to know who he was, and Thomas answered, "I am Thomas. God sent me."

Ann remembers Thomas holding his right hand up and faced Ann. She could feel the heat coming from his hand and felt her legs coming out from her, and she fell to the floor. As Ann was laying there, she saw a strong white light that was traveling through her body, mind, and heart – as though there was something supernatural that was occurring. She passed out and when she awoke – Gary was leaning over her asking was she alright, but Thomas was gone. Ann crawled over to the telephone and called her doctor and told him that she was cancer free, and of course – the doctor thought that the stress and fear made her delusional.

Story Of An Angel

Before Ann went through her surgery, she had a biopsy test. The test came back clean, and the doctor did not understand what was happening, and thus sent her labs for further testing.

There has been no relapse regarding Ann's cancer. Ann was hesitant to talk about the encounter with Thomas because people to include her children would think that she was crazy – lost it. However, Ann's doctor claims that he had "witnessed a miracle as well."[51]

"The emphasis on angels as divine intermediaries, theologians worry, just creates a greater distance from an ever more abstract God. And to the extent that angels are always benign spirits, it evades any reckoning with the struggle between good and evil." Tony Kushner, says that if we are to solve problems on earth, that we must do it ourselves, and is troubled that angels appear to some people and not others.

I agree with Westerhoff – although it may appear that everyone has different levels of faith. While some have high levels of spiritual faith – perhaps some have no faith at all and the cause why some have different levels of angelic experiences.

"For all those who say they have had some direct experience of angels, no proof is necessary; for those predisposed doubt angels existence, no proof is possible. And for those in the mystified

---

[51] Gibbs, Nancy, and Sam Allis. "Angels among us. (Cover story)." *Time* 142, no. 27 (December 27, 1993): 56. *MAS Ultra - School Edition.* The story about Ann Cannady came from tis source.

middle, there is often a growing desire to be persuaded. If heaven is willing to sing to us, it is little to ask we be ready to listen." [52]

In these troubled times that we encounter today, many people have a little faith, and again, some have more faith than others, but who are we to judge whether or not an individual has had an encounter with an angel. First, we were not there to witness the encounter – and perhaps should not doubt the spiritual encounters that others have/had with their angels.

Conclusion

We read about a unique story about a woman that was distraught because she was diagnosed with cancer, and her husband went to the same occurrence with his previous x wife and didn't think he would be able to go through it again with his current wife. An angel appeared to her and told her that she was cured. In addition to that, the doctor was amazed that she showed no relapse of any cancer.

I suggest that we all have different trials and pains that are not the same as others. Each trial is different, and we should not assume that this occurrence with the angel did not happen. Nor should we be in disagreement that her cancer showed no signs of relapse because she said the angel told her so.

---

[52] Gibbs, Nancy, and Sam Allis. "Angels among us. (Cover story)." *Time* 142, no. 27 (December 27, 1993): 56. *MAS Ultra - School Edition.*

One's faith is a determining factor regarding angelic experiences. *No faith* is equivalent to nothing spiritual occurring in your life. Spiritual faith is equivalent to blessings and occurrences that are often viewed as being nonexistence from one that has no faith at all.

RELATIONSHIP BETWEEN GOD - ANGELS AND HUMANS

―――――⋅⸙⋅―――――

"Enter ye at the straight gate: for wide is the gate, and broad is the way, that leadeth to destruction, and many there be which go in thereat: 14- Because straight is the gate, and narrow is the way, which leadeth unto life, and few there be that find it." (Matthew 7: 13-14) [53]

I am certain that every one of us has an inner voice that speaks to us – gives us our next task and helps resolve the things in our lives that hinder us. That inner voice gives us solutions to solve problems and keep us on the right path regarding living gracefully and not losing our souls to Satan's advantage.

---

[53] Felder, Cain Hope. *The Original African Heritage Study Bible* (King James Version). {Judson Press, 2007}. Mathew 7: 13-14, p. 1338.

I am also certain that the little voice that leads us on the straight and narrow road – is our personal guardian angel; that inner voice that acts as a mediator between ourselves and God.

There is nothing in this world that God does not know. He knows what we are thinking, and what we are going to do before we do it and that all has to do with giving us free will of choice. By God giving us the free will to *choose*, it is good that we have a guardian angel to help make us make right the choices.

For example, you are walking inside a grocery store, and someone that you see in front of you drops a twenty dollar bill on the aisle floor. That instant voice that resonates inside your head that says, that they've dropped money on the floor – is the angel within you; the angel giving you good advice. For some, they may wish to ignore that good voice and adhere to the voice that says, "pick it up and keep it, you're short on your bills this month, and that twenty dollars would be a big help." Those people are listening to the wrong demonic inner voice and or their evil desires.

God created the holy angels to act as his *mediators* and *messengers*, and carry his motivations and beauties to us and bring back our prayers and sacrifices directly to Him.[54]

---

[54] Hammenstede, Albert. 1945. "The holy angels and we." *Orate Fratres* 19, no. 9: 400-406. *ATLA Religion Database with ATLASerials*, EBSCO*host*, p.400.

God's good grace is vital to the betterment of men. Angels are an asset to the human race, for without them, we all would at some time or another make bad choices and make God sad.

"Every angel is an interpreter. It is Hermes who flashes in the dark cracks between different realms. Communication between these realms is not self-evident. It is an angel who mediates them."[55]

People often explain occurrences, and for them may appear to be a miracle(s), and I believe that angels are the watchers of our hearts.

In many cases, we are taught by having occasional experiences – which God is always watching over us, and showing us alternative ways that his love is always more prevalent for one to be a decent human being. Angels show us alternative methods to be productive.

The best advice one can give to another is to start listening to your inner voice – *the voice that directs you to make good on decisions.* That inner voice – I have c concluded is our guardian angel. *The bad inner voice that directs us to do the opposite of good is a demon.* Many are not prone to respond to our inner voice – but should be aware *that the inner voice that directs us to be close to God and do the right things in life is indeed our guardian angel.*

I find that it is very important to give names of the important angels as described in the book of Enoch that are in the Apocrypha. One might suggest that because the book of Enoch is one of the

---

[55] Bayer, Oswald. "Angels Are Interpreters." *Lutheran Quarterly* 13, no. 3 (1999 1999): 271-284. *ATLA Religion Database with ATLASerials*, EBSCO*host, p. 274.*

rejected text, that the scripture that it provides is worthless.

However, I will suggest that all books concerning scripture have significance. I find all text are worthy of its substance, because, in short, it is a reflection of God.

The names of the holy angels who watch, are as follows:

1. Uriel – the holy angel who is over the world regarding turmoil, as well as terror.
2. Raphael – the holy angel who is over the spirits of men
3. Raguel - the holy angel that takes retaliation on the world of the achievers
4. Michael – one of the holy angels that set over the virtues of mankind as well as chaos
5. Seroquel – the holy angel that resides over spirits, who sins in the spirit
6. Gabriel - the holy angel that oversees the serpents, paradise, as well as the cherubim
7. Remiel – the holy angel that God has set over those who rise[56]

Conclusion

I am convinced that the voice we hear within our thoughts is the voice of our guardian angel directing us in a righteous manner. Our guardian angel is that angel that works directly under God's

---

[56] Lumpkin, Joseph. The Apocrypha: Including Books from the Bible. {Joseph Lumpkin, 2009}, p. 386,387. The book of Enoch.

grace, and, therefore, wants and directs us to stay in good grace with God at all times, and we should listen to our guardian angel as opposed to not listening, which could lead us out of God's grace.

Our guardian angel is a mediator between ourselves and God, and will often show us another course of action for our problems. Often it is when we steer away from the Lord and do things on our time, and our way is when we fail miserably. Listen to your guardian angel. He is always available to help us. That's their job.

ANGELS AND CHILDREN

We often look at our children and our grandchildren as angels, especially our grandchildren. Our children and grandchildren are or were at one time – new to this world. Some children at a young age – often have good dreams about angels after being told stories by grown adults. At least, I had dreams of good angels.

Angels have become a significant special part of the relationship with our children and with God. The angels being the intermediary.

We are bound together with angels, and the angel is the concrete way that God becomes present in various instances (Bayer, 1999, p.280).

The world of angels and children are wonderful – in that the impossible becomes possible in this world and beyond as we grow.[57]

If God loves children, then it is quite obvious that his angels will love children just as God does. Psalm 127: 3-4, says "Lo, children

---

[57] Steimle, Edmund Augustus. 1969. "Children and angels." *Union Seminary Quarterly Review* 24, no. 3: 265-271. *ATLA Religion Database with ATLASerials*, EBSCO*host*, p. 265.

are a heritage of the Lord; and the fruit of the womb is his reward. As arrows are in the hand of the mighty man; so are children of the youth."[58]

The Bible contains 66 books and over 35 different authors from different times. The Bible takes account that Jesus loved children and says, "See that you do not despise one of these little ones; for I tell you that in heaven their angels always behold the face of my Father, which is in heaven." [59]

Edmund Augustus Steimle, suggests that angels are not only alive but also an indication that God is in our presence, and for us comprehend that veracity, we have to become like children.

"It takes children to make a Christmas, nor in the same sense that it's easy for children to believe in the miraculous, the bizarre, and the world of angels, but in the same sense perhaps that the child has the capacity for wonder and delight in the presence of the mystery and the unpredictability of life," [60]

---

[58] Felder, Cain Hope. *The Original African Heritage Study Bible* (King James Version). {Judson Press, 2007}, Psalms 127:3-4 was taken from this Bible.

[59] Steimle, Edmund Augustus. 1969. "Children and angels." *Union Seminary Quarterly Review* 24, no. 3: 265-271. *ATLA Religion Database with ATLASerials*, EBSCO*host, p266*. Here Steimle concludes with this entry that there are guardian angels that are with us and that there are other orders of angels as well.

[60] Steimle, Edmund Augustus. 1969. "Children and angels." *Union Seminary Quarterly Review* 24, no. 3: 265-271. *ATLA Religion Database with ATLASerials*, EBSCO*host, p. 268*.

On several occasions – my nine-year-old granddaughter has said some unique things to me that made me think how did she know that? Her suggestion/comment had changed my whole outlook on a subject that we were discussing at the time. Her suggestion/comment(s) had to have come from someone other than herself, and I am convinced that perhaps it was her guardian angel.

Although she attends a very good private Christian school that teaches right from wrong, I strongly feel that her comments; even though they may have come from her mouth, it could have well been her angel assisting her with her thoughts.

There is no way that a nine-year-old can comment as she has in the past without the help of something more thoughtful and powerful than herself.

Our children & grandchildren have angels that often speak for them to rattle our adult thought process back on a Christian scale, but according to Susan Garrett – "angels are supporting players and bit characters who seldom steal the limelight. They are often essential to the unfolding story. Because angels can appear invisible guise and converse with human beings, they assist in the portrayal of an invisible, ineffable deity." [61]

Angels act as mediators in the Old Testament & New Testament – why wouldn't they act on our behalf, when we need them to interact and act as an intermediary between parties today? I am

---

[61] Garrett, Susan R. 2009. *"Jesus and the angels." Word & World* 29, no. 2: 162-169. *ATLA Religion Database with ATLASerials*, EBSCOhost

convinced that angels give us the advice we need to remain in the good graces of God.

An important note: According to Lawrence Osborn, "Angels have never been a major element in evangelical theology." So, with that being said, it is important for us to focus on the things that occur and surround us in our everyday life – that do not have an explanation that otherwise may be explained by a theologian.[62]

Another important note from Lawrence Osborn is that he also suggests, "As God's courtiers, the angels are also God's servants; God's ministers."

What an important gesture to confirm that God loves us so much that he has servants(angels in particular) that minister to us in unique ways to make sure that we stay in his grace and live according to his commandments.

Our ultimate joy will be with God and the rest of his children in heaven. Ministering can come directly from our children and grandchildren that God sees as his loving children.

Conclusion

Angels are a significant part of a child's life, especially during Christmas season. In many instances, we often hear our children and grandchildren say things that we know for sure that it must

---

[62] Osborn, Lawrence. "Entertaining Angels: Their Place in Contemporary Theology." *Tyndale Bulletin* 45, no. 2 (November 1994): 273-296. *ATLA Religion Database with ATLASerials*, EBSCO*host*.

have been someone other than him of herself that came up with a particular thought during a conversation. I suggest that perhaps that was their guardian angel steering us back in the right direction (God's grace). There may not be an explanation of a lot of occurrences, but one must know that God knows everything, and often, our children are here to do God's work so we can watch and learn as well.

Parts three and four will discuss in great detail – about Satan/Lucifer, and his demons.

SATAN

Who and what is Satan? Satan is best described in the book of Genesis, like the serpent that tempted Eve to eat from the tree of knowledge in the Garden of Eden, after God forbid them to eat the fruit from that tree (the tree of knowledge). God told Adam and Eve that they could eat from any tree in the Garden of Eden, but they must not eat from the tree of knowledge, or they will surely die. Satan, the clever deceiver that he is told Eve a lie - that if she ate the fruit from the tree of knowledge, she would not die. [63]

People often associate evil with Satan, and according to J. Russell, he attributes that Elaine Pagels, a professor of Religion at Princeton University, suggests, "What fascinates us about Satan is the way he expresses qualities that go beyond what we ordinarily recognize as human." [64]

---

[63] Felder, Cain Hope. *The Original African Heritage Study Bible* (King James Version). {Judson Press, 2007}, p. 6.

[64] Russell, Jeffrey Burton. "Getting Satan behind Us." *First Things* 57, (November 1995): 40-45. *ATLA Religion Database with ATLASerials*, EBSCO*host*

Satan was a light bearer that was considered the perfect angel as well as the chief angel of the cherub angels. Satan was born intelligent, and powerful, and a very wise angel.

Ezekiel 28:12-15-16 describes Satan best:

> "Son of man, take up a lamentation upon the king of Tyrus, and say unto him, Thus saith the Lord God: Thou sealest up the sum, full of wisdom, and perfect in beauty. Thou hast been in Eden the garden of God; every precious stone was thy covering, the sardius, topaz, and the diamond, and then beryl, the onyx, and the jasper, the sapphire, the emerald, and the carbuncle, and gold. The workmanship of thy tabrets and thy pipes was prepared in thee in the day that thou was created." [65]

When one reads Ezekiel chapter 28, one will find that because Satan had everything, regarding beauty, he became corrupted, and became nothing, because of his pride.

When one thinks about the events that took place in Genesis chapter 3, we must consider that it was knowledge that ultimately destroyed and cursed man. Even today, we are suffering at the hands of Satan for thinking we know better than God, and often change

---

[65] Felder, Cain Hope. *The Original African Heritage Study Bible* (King James Version). {Judson Press, 2007}, Ezekiel chapter 28, p. 1217.

Exegetical Study of Angels & Demons

things that are against God's commandments – to suit our daily lives – neglecting God, and doing as we well, please. Satan being the prize angel and fell short because of his pride, should be an example for us to follow, regarding remaining humble to God, our creator.

We must be vigilant and forever reminded that, because of Satan's temptation – we must be the wise human beings on this earth where Satan is considered the prince according to Jesus (John 12:31).

We should also at the same time enjoy the things on this earth (Wisdom of Solomon 2:7)[66] and be aware of the snare of Satan – for he(Satan) is the one that seeks to destroy man.

Being aware that Satan attacks out thoughts, and from that, we often make bad choices without even giving our state of affairs a second thought, but afterward – we realize that we made a bad choice. Again being vigilant and remembering that Satan is the deceiver that is always lurking to destroy mankind. According to Boa & Bowman Jr, Satan is limited regarding what he can know about us – unlike God, because the devil does not know our hearts (1 Kings 8:39). Satan can only get a good idea regarding what we are thinking or feeling by watching us. [67]

---

[66] Lumpkin, Joseph. *The Apocrypha: Including Books from the Bible.* {Joseph Lumpkin, 2009}.
"Come, therefore, let us enjoy the good things that exist, and make use of the creation to the full as in youth." P. 296.

[67] Boa, Kenneth D & Bowman, Robert M Jr. *Sense & Nonsense about Angels & Demons.* {Zondervan, 2007}, p. 113 – advises that Satan does not know our hearts.

Peter Kreeft suggests that Satan and the other demons are by nature, spirits, and was created by God, and was for the most part – good, but fell into a sinful nature by their free will, and are "eternally damned."[68]

Also, Kreeft (1995) suggests that Satan prefers for us to underestimate his authority over us and be ever forgetful that he is the enemy. "We wrestle not against flesh and blood but principalities and powers of wickedness in high places" (Eph 6).

We must also remember that Satan was a light-bearer, and he was once the highest angel next to God, but his rebellion got him kicked out of heaven. Satan as well as other demons fought in heaven because Satan thought he was better than God.

That is a good case where one can see where pride interferes with one's judgment of good and evil, and in Satan's case, he surely made an incorrect decision by showing his pride towards God.

I find the following story from the Qur'an interesting, to say the least, and tells the story of Satan's rebellion this way:

> "Then verily We {Allah} shall narrate unto them {the event} with knowledge, for verily we were not absent {when it came to pass}…And we created you {mankind}, then fashioned you, then told the angels: Fall ye prostrate before Adam! And they

---

[68] Kreeft, Peter. *Angels and Demons, What do we really know about them?* {San Francisco: Ignatius Press, 1995}, p. 111.

fell prostrate, all save Iblis {Allah} said: What hindered thee that thou didst fall prostrate when I bade thee? {Iblis} said: "I am better than him. Thou created me from fire while he didst create of mud. He {Allah} said: Then go down hence! It is not for thee to show pride here, so –go forth! Lo, thou are of these degraded" (Surah V11, 7-13).

In the Christian account God told Satan and his angels that he was going to create man but also to incarnate himself in a man – in Jesus and the other angels refused to accept this, and or bow to a God of flesh and blood. In all of the verses – the sin is pride. "I will not serve." [69]

Perhaps the angels fell from heaven at the time that the earth was created or very soon afterward during what is called "matter." The matter was more than likely created some eighteen billion years ago according to Kreeft and was probably the time when the angels were also created as well – during the time of the big bang theory. There is no measuring stick or clock that can suggest the date, time, or hour that this might have occurred.

There was a Cultural-Development study of 120 participants from an Evangelical Presbyterian church in Washington DC that

---

[69] Kreeft, Peter. *Angels and Demons, What do we really know about them?* {San Francisco: Ignatius Press, 1995}, p. 119. Shows how Satan and his angels refused to obey God and thus was forced out of heaven.

was given, where the majority of the participants resided, that suggested that 62% of American adults believe in the devil, and 82% of Americans believe in God. [70] The ages of this study ranged from 13-57 years of age.

This study suggests that although many of us believe in God – fewer believe that the devil exist.

Conclusion

The first encounter with Satan was when he tempted Eve into eating fruit from the forbidden tree of knowledge that God told them(Adam and Eve) that they could eat from any tree in the garden, except the specific tree(tree of knowledge).

Satan, because he did not like God's creation (humans), he decided to tempt Eve, by telling her that she would not die, when God told her just the opposite, that if she were to eat from the tree of knowledge, that she would surely die.

We have considered that knowledge can be detrimental if not used in a correct manner. For example, a pastor can preach about different words in Greek and Hebrew that are found in the Bible, but can talk over the heads of the people listening, in his or her congregation.

---

[70] Jensen, Lene Arnett. "Conceptions of God and the Devil across the Lifespan: A Cultural-Developmental Study of Religious Liberals and Conservatives." *Journal for the Scientific Study of Religion* 48, no. 1 (March 2009): 121-145. *Academic Search Premier*, EBSCO*host* (accessed November 17, 2015).

The people in the congregation, either do not understand or perhaps they may consider taking a nap during that portion of the sermon. Too much knowledge can work for or against you.

Let's consider if Eve ignored Satan and didn't eat from the tree, would life be different for humans? Today, would we be living in paradise here on earth? We are often told that we are all born into sin, and that was due to the sin that occurred in the Garden of Eden, with Adam and Eve and Satan, being the deceiver.

We must continue to reframe from temptation, but at the same time enjoy this life that God gave us. This life was meant to be enjoyed, even though Satan's job is to deceive and destroy, and even though we are tempted does not mean that Satan can read our thoughts.

J. Russell suggested that according to E. Pagel that the first place that one should look at when it comes to recognizing evil is to look at ourselves first. [71]

Satan cannot read our thoughts, but what he can do is observe us and only get an idea of what we are thinking.

Having differences with a loved one can be a very sobering experience, but we are reminded that when this happens, we are not arguing with the person (flesh and blood), but we are arguing with the powers and principalities as described in Ephesians 6.

---

[71] Russell, Jeffrey Burton. "Getting Satan behind Us." *First Things* 57, (November 1995): 40-45. *ATLA Religion Database with ATLASerials*, EBSCO*host:* We must consider looking at the evil that is done to us and by us, is to recognize the evil within ourselves.

Continue to follow the Lord, because Satan rebelled against God because he didn't want to share the love God had with us because we were flesh and blood. Remember, that Satan and his demons do exist, and be wary of their trickery, because they lurk about the earth seeking to destroy, and devour.

PART 3

DEMONS

Is there a difference between Satan and demons? Yes, of course. The difference is that Satan is the chief of operations, and demons are his assistants.

Should we be afraid of demons? Yes, we should be afraid of demons, according to Kreeft. Demons can tempt us through our imagination or feelings, and can deceive us with false revelation. Many times I have heard people discuss matters about ancient religious doctrines that did not include Yeshua/Hebrew or Jesus/English, and or God and the Holy Trinity.

These discussions can go on for hours into days, and all the time, I'm thinking about how twisted their theories have become and appear to have demonic authority/ control, in the subject matter.

There are people (including those in the ministry) that are teaching false doctrines and swear by it, and of course – Satan and his demons are responsible for the confusion and spreading of lies, as it pertains to the true church doctrines of the Trinity.

Exegetical Study of Angels & Demons

2 Peter 2:1-3, teaches us that there will be false prophets amongst us, and their greed will exploit you with false words, and according to David Moshier, there will be plenty of them that will be amongst us. [72]

Demons are considered being the lower class of bad, or fallen angels. In the view of Christians, demons are evil, and just like Satan, are fallen angels that chose pride over submission to God. [73]

Demons have a history of tampering with the affairs of humans lives, and they are really good deceivers and tricksters as well, according to Gailey. The djinn of Arabian lore, suggests that demons were the original inhabitants of the earth that were convicted by God, for humans. [74]

"The Spirit clearly says that in later times some will abandon the faith and follow deceiving spirits and things taught by demons." (Timothy 4:1) – "As an intimidator of God, Satan seeks to use his doctrine to deceive believers into giving up on their faith; sometimes he uses ministers and teachers in the church to spread his lies" (Warren Wiersbe). [75]

---

[72] Moshier, David. *Satan is no Angel (and never was)*. {David Moshier, 2013}, p. 62.

[73] Guiley, Rosemary Ellen. *The Encyclopedia of Demons and Demonology*. {Checkmark Books, 2009}.

[74] Guiley, Rosemary Ellen. *The Encyclopedia of Demons and Demonology*. {Checkmark Books, 2009}.

[75] Bethany House Publishers. *Everything the Bible says about Angels and Demons*. {Bloomington Minnesota: Bethany House Publishers, 2012}, p 114 – talks about how Satan deceives by using false doctrines.

Many chose to follow Satan and his demons, as opposed to accepting God. Others have joined colts that are widespread in the United States and probably numbered in the hundreds, according to Medway. [76]

When the movie Exorcist came to the movie screens, at some point, I had serious doubts about exorcisms that the Catholic Church swears by, but research has proven that exorcist occurs quite frequently around the world. Kreeft suggests that demons can possess us only in the event where we invite them in.[77] Playing board games such as Ouija, and the use of tarot cards and cardboard tarot games can open the doors for demonic interferences. As Fred Dickason suggest, Satan is real, and these three words should be addressed when dealing with Satan, and they are, to begin with being properly understood, summarize our responsibilities by recalling, fighting and have faith in oneself. [78]

Keep in mind that Satan and his demons are great deceivers and can predict the future and have access to insider information as well.

Deuteronomy 18: 10-14 says:

> "There shall not be found among you any one that maketh his son or his daughter to pass through the fire,

---

[76] Medway, Gareth J. *Lure of the sinister: The unnatural history of Satanism.* University Press, 2001.

[77] Kreeft, Peter. *Angels and Demons, What do we really know about them?* {San Francisco: Ignatius Press, 1995}, p.114.

[78] Dickason, C. Fred. *Angels – Elect &Evil.* {Moody Publishers, 1975}, p. 216.

> or that useth divination, or an observer of times, or an enhancer, or a witch, or a charmer, or a consulter with familiar spirits, or a wizard, or a necromancer. For all that do these things are an abomination unto the Lord: and because of these abominations the Lord thy God doth drive them out from before thee. Thou shall be perfect with the Lord thy God. For these nations, which thou shalt possess, hearkened unto observers of times, and to diviners; but as for thee, the Lord thy God hath not suffered thee so to do." [79]

That being said, we must be mindful not to invite Satan and his demons into our daily lives by not letting our children play with board games such as the Ouija board, or tarot cards, the cards that fortune tellers use to tell you about your future. All things that are in spiritual nature that does not include the Trinity should be subdued completely.

"In magical lore, some demons have good dispositions, and some do not. They offer humans gifts of wealth, knowledge, power and pleasure – but always at a price. The greatest price is one's

---

[79] Felder, Cain Hope. *The Original African Heritage Study Bible* (King James Version). {Judson Press, 2007}. Deuteronomy 18, p. 316.

soul." [80] God authorizes evil to exist under the path of an archfiend (Satan).[81]

We must take into consideration, that Satan is very limited in his powers, as well as his activities. Thus, Satan can only do what God permits him to do, as described in Job 1: 12, 2:6, and 1 John 4:4. [82]

From personal experiences, and having witnessed several incidents; I suggest that many of us that are in the ministry, are frequently attacked by demons, more often than others (lay persons). We cannot remain ignorant regarding the devices that Satan uses against us, and must always be aware of his strategies (2 Co 2:11; Eph 6:11). [83]

We must be aware that many of the things we do to others as well as to ourselves can cause spiritual and psychological deformities, and that is to include the use of mind altering drugs. [84]

Greek philosophers during the seventh century suggest that "Angels who fell from heaven busy themselves about the air and the earth and are no longer able to rise to the realms of the heavens.

---

[80] Guiley, Rosemary Ellen. *The Encyclopedia of Demons and Demonology.* {Checkmark Books, 2009}.

[81] Guiley, Rosemary Ellen. *The Encyclopedia of Demons and Demonology.* {Checkmark Books, 2009}.

[82] Dickason, C. Fred. *Angels – Elect &Evil.* {Moody Publishers, 1975}.Dickason, C. Fred. *Angels – Elect &Evil.* {Moody Publishers, 1975}, p.216.

[83] Dickason, C. Fred. *Angels – Elect &Evil.* {Moody Publishers, 1975}, p.217.

[84] remmel, William C. "Satan - the dark side." *Iliff Review* 42, no. 1 (1985 1985): 3-12. *ATLA Religion Database with ATLASerials,* EBSCO*host*

The souls of the giants are the demons who wonder about the world. Both angels and demons produce movements – demons movements which are akin to the natures they received, and angels' movements which are akin to the lust with which they are possessed." [85]

Conclusion

- The difference between Satan and demons is that Satan is the boss, where his demons are his workers that often tempt us through our imaginations and feelings.
- People that serve in the ministry are more prone to attacks than those lay persons, by spreading false doctrines as well as lies that do not belong to church doctrine.
- According to Warren Wiersbe, Satan seeks to use his doctrine and often will use ministers as well as teachers, to spread his lies.
- When we experiment with board games and Tarot cards, we are opening doors for Satan to step in our lives and wreak any havoc he chooses to stow upon us, and therefore, we should refrain from any witchcraft logics. At first, one might suggest that nothing is going to happen to them by playing these games, but after time spirits will contact you and become a nuisance.
- We must also remember that good spirits will obey God and not contact humans in this manner, only the bad spirits/demons will.

---

[85] Giulea, Dragoş-Andrei. "The Watchers' Whispers: Athenagoras's Legatio 25, 1-3 and the Book of the Watchers." *Vigiliae Christianae* 61, no. 3 (August 2007): 258-281. *Academic Search Premier.*

ETHICAL AND MORAL DIVISION AGAINST GOD

*G*reek philosophers in the seventh century, tell us that fallen angels wonder about the world producing movements that are similar to the covetousness in which they are possessed.

Our attempts on this earth are to make it to heaven, but the fallen angels – like Satan became annoyed and full of pride. The fallen angels and were kicked out of heaven and bound in hell, to face their eternal judgment.

Matthew 25:41 says, "Then shall he also say unto them on the left hand, Depart from me, ye cursed, into everlasting fire, prepared for the devil and his angels." [86]

One must recognize that a hell is a place of everlasting torment while heaven is a place of love and joy as we have read in the scriptures. Robert Louis Wilken suggests the scriptures begin with the

---

[86] Felder, Cain Hope. *The Original African Heritage Study Bible* (King James Version). {Judson Press, 2007}, Matthew 25:41, p. 1425.

Exegetical Study of Angels & Demons

creation of the world as well as human beings and ends with a door that is open to heaven. [87]

There are repercussions when *anyone*, to include angels – fail to obey God. In the case of fallen angels, they became envious of humans and sided with Satan, perhaps because they thought for some strange reason because Satan was once a top angel in rank – he knew more than God himself, which the old saying goes; misery loves company.

Revelation 12; 7-9 tells us (paraphrasing) that there was a war in heaven, where Michael and his angels had a fight with Satan, and they fought back, but was cast out of heaven and landed here on earth, along with his angels, where they are today.

Also, the fallen angels fit into two classes of angels that are free and those angels that are bound.

Satan is given a seat in the governments of this world that authorizes his evil – regarding maintaining his rulership. [88]

Dan.10:13, and in Eph.6:12, refers to Satan having a world system of his government – regarding his world systems. Satan's powers are practically ever-present and cause the fall of the human race (Genesis 3). Satan's judgment in the Garden of Eden and was very well accomplished on the cross (John 12: 31 – 33). Satan's powers were second to God (Ezek.28:11-16) and were only a

---

[87] Wilken, Robert L. "*With angels and archangels.*" *Pro Ecclesia* 10, no. 4 (September 2001): 460-474. *ATLA Religion Database with ATLASerials*, EBSCO*host, p. 461.*

[88] Felder, Cain Hope. *The Original African Heritage Study Bible* (King James Version). {Judson Press, 2007}, commentary footnote, p. 1795.

creature, which is omnipotence and omniscience, and has divine powers that are permitted by God. [89]

Satan continues to be a nuisance to all men, and his plans are to destroy as many humans as he possibly can by tempting us to do the things that are against the word of God. The unsaved will more than likely be cast down with Satan when he is sent to his demise. The saved will be tempted. Satan will destroy their testimony as well as their physical life (Eph. 6:11-18), according to Elwell, 2001.

However, in the end, Satan and his demons will attempt to gain control of the world, and will subsequently be kept in the void for one thousand years. After the one thousand years, they will make another attempt to fight God, and again will loose and will be cast into the lake of fire for eternity.[90]

Conclusion

The Greek philosophers in the seventh centuries tell us that the fallen angels wander around the world seeking to destroy, and our attempts to live graciously on this earth is to make it ultimately into heaven.

---

[89] Elwell, Walter A. *Evangelical Dictionary of Theology*. Baker Academic, 2001, p. 1054.

[90] Elwell, Walter A. *Evangelical Dictionary of Theology*. Baker Academic, 2001, p. 1054.

Repercussions prevail to anyone that disobeys the commandments of God and fall short of the glory of God, and because Satan and his demons disobeyed God, they were cast out of heaven and fell here on earth to torture us into temptation and thus fall short of the glory of God. Satan's ultimate goal is to destroy as many human lives as possible because he knows that his time here on earth is very short. He will be void for one thousand years and thus, will return to fight another battle with God and lose and eventually be cast into the lake of fire.

SATANISM

"The origins of Christian accusations of diabolical or satanic witchcraft first arose around A.D. 900. Over the next six centuries, criteria for identifying Satanist were formed and finally codified in the *Malleus Maleficarum* (The Hammer of Witches; 1486)." [91]

In the context of today's society, there are groups that gather together to commit crimes of violence to innocent people. It is certainly true that Satan is the prince or ruler of the world we live in today (John 12:31, 14:30).

In today's world, we are surrounded by demonic experiences and temptations. If one is not careful, he or she can easily get caught up in one of Satan's tricks. People often experiment with satanic rituals, out of curiosity, and before they know it, something that was once experimental, all of a sudden becomes a reality.

---

[91] Elwell, Walter A. *Evangelical Dictionary of Theology*. Baker Academic, 2001, p. 1055.

Exegetical Study of Angels & Demons

Satanic groups often become obsolete after periods of activity, and in most cases become difficult regarding their measurements of active activity. However, there is evidence that suggests that family traditions of Satanism come from generation to generation.[92] Satanism is the devotion to Satan, and or his forces of darkness, and there was little-known evidence that organized Satanism existed before the seventeenth century.[93]

Modern Satanism began in the 1960's in the United States. Anton Lavey was the founder of the Church of Satanism in San Francisco California.

The Catholic Church was condemning priest that were subverting magical powers of holy mass for evil purposes. The Order of the Knights Templar and other rival religious sects that were enemies of the Catholic Church were accused of devil worshipping, witchcraft, and crimes of unorthodoxy, and confessed after being tortured.[94]

Also, there was an ethical fear that presided in the United States in the 1980's as well as the 1990's, because of religious cults. These

---

[92] Guiley, Rosemary Ellen. *The Encyclopedia of Demons and Demonology.* {Checkmark Books, 2009}, p.227.

[93] Guiley, Rosemary Ellen. *The Encyclopedia of Demons and Demonology.* {Checkmark Books, 2009}, p. 224.

[94] Guiley, Rosemary Ellen. *The Encyclopedia of Demons and Demonology.* {Checkmark Books, 2009}, p. 224.

cults are perceived as people that were mentally ill, and evil, and were viewed as a threat to society as well as one's family life. [95]

Anton LaVey's Church of Satan as well as other smaller Satanist organizations, typically forbid any harmful rituals. However, there were those times where perhaps a ritual was acted out, and lives are lost, due to the extreme acting out of the rituals (Reichert, Jenny, and James T Richardson, 2012, p. 49).

Drugs can also be a big influence regarding acting out Satanic ritualistic roles. Hallucinogenic drugs such as LSD, PCP, and the most recent drug, synthetic marijuana.

Carlie Manson was responsible for over 30 killings in the California area in the late 1960's, and that is to include actress Sharon Tate, along with a host of other Hollywood celebrities. Manson was never found guilty of the crimes but because he had a hold on his so called "family" that performed the killings by way of mind control and the use of drugs, like mushrooms as well as LSD.

"During the cult scare of the 1970's and 1980's, the media presented cult leaders as charismatic charlatans who conned followers out of their free will.

Cult members were weak, brainwashed individuals who were tricked into participating" (Reichert, Jenny, and James T Richardson, 2012, p. 51), and again drugs can play a big role regarding recruitment efforts.

---

[95] Reichert, Jenny, and James T Richardson. "Decline of a moral panic: a social psychological and socio-legal examination of the current status of Satanism." *Nova Religion* 16, no. 2, p. 48.

With this being said, there were various court cases where there were allegations of Satanic associations, regarding homicides, as well as child abusers.

However, the courts hold that evidence of Satanic immersion is superlative to proving motive as well as the intent (Reichert, Jenny, and James T Richardson, 2012, p. 54).

Conclusion

Satanic witchcraft began around 900A.D while Satanist were forming to begin around 1486. We should ever be reminded of John 12:31, and 14:30, (paraphrasing) that Satan is the ruler of this world that we live in today. Fear in the United States began to take shape around the 70's, 80's, and 90's, due to religious cults that began to appear.

Demonic experiences from Satanist groups can easily be conformed to a belief system, only if one is not careful and mindful of the world that we live in today, that is, filled with those things that are not Christ-like, or scriptural based.

Drugs can play a significant role regarding brainwashing one into thinking into the Satanist belief systems. Satanist are dedicated to the beliefs of Satan himself, and we should always keep in mind, that no matter who starts a Satanist or cult movement, our fight is not with the movement, but our fight is with Satan himself.

CLOSE ANALYSIS OF SATAN AND HIS DEMONS

For the individual that lives on this earth and fearful of living, because Satan is the ruler of this earth – John 12:31, and 14:30. We should rely heavily on our faith, reason because the faithful know that when we resist the temptation(s) from Satan, and his demons, our Father in heaven will reward us with everlasting life. Also, for those of us who believe in *eternal life*, it is a sign of the hope we have in another life that is even better than this one." [96]

The apostle John reminds us that we need to focus on Christ and what we will gain in the new life by doing so. In chapter 4 in the book of Revelation, he (John) describes a vision regarding seeing angels and elders that were surrounding God, while God is sitting

---

[96] Arnold, Johann Christoph. *"Exploring Heaven & HELL."* USA Today Magazine 131, no. 2692 (January 2003): 58. Academic Search Premier, EBSCOhost, p.58.

upon a throne. In chapter 5, it is suggested that Jesus holds the book that has the certainty and importance of history.[97]

The minute we forget that Satan is the ruler of this earth is the minute when we begin to fall short of the glory and grace of God. Satan and his demons prowl the earth looking to wreak havoc on human beings and destroying anything they love.

Take a deep look at the current society that we live in today, and we will find that is full of disease, drugs, suicide, drunkenness, and homosexuality. People today, do as they please, and have no regards for God while they do as they please, and have pleasure in sinning. There always seems to be an answer to every sin, and why their sin is not a sin, and often it is the Christian that is always shunned for bringing God into a conversation, and correcting bad behaviors via the scriptures. There is a lot of compromise in scripture that people and the church leaders claim (makeup) to satisfy their sins. God's word is written and should not be compromised to suit the sinner, and his or her sins.

Satan has manipulated the minds of people, having them think that God does not care about them and that their lives are worthless. Suicide has become more rampant, especially when our youth are involved, and are suffering from some form of depression, or mental illness. Satan's manipulation, just adds fuel to the fire, when one does not include Christ in his or her affairs.

---

[97] Felder, Cain Hope. *True to our Native Land*. Fortress Press, 2007, p. 524.

Another example of Satan's manipulation is the Charleston South Carolina shootings that occurred during Bible study inside an AME church back in June of 2015. A young man invited himself into an African American church and began shooting the pastor as well as other members while they were attending the Bible study.

According to reports on the incident, the young man was influenced by white supremacy philosophy, that prey on people that do not agree with their philosophy, regarding hating others, because of different qualities, such as one's race being an initial factor.

Satan is the primary reason for the manipulation of the minds of people. Satan can install fear, especially in the minds of those that are not following the word of God.

One primary purpose of this book is to show the goodness of angels and how they work for the good of humanity in our lives, and how Satan and his demons work tirelessly towards wreaking havoc and creating turmoil in the human life experience.

The question remains; do angels exist, bad angels and good angels, and is their purpose to serve humanity whether it be regarding doing good or bad for humanity?

Angels transfer messages from earth to God, and visa-verse, and God himself makes final judgments and or decisions, regarding certain events that angels transfer back to God. God has the final say in all matters (paraphrasing) (Acts 10:24).

The reason for the prior statement, regarding relaying messages, takes one back to the beginning when an angel advised God what he had seen.

When Adam and Eve were tossed out of the Garden of Eden, and how he saw both Adam and Eve grieving, and God told the angel to assist them and not destroy them for their disobedience.

Conclusion

We have acknowledged that John 12:31, says that Satan is the ruler of this earth, and one should rely on his or her faith, regarding being able to resist the temptations that Satan and his demons may bring in our path(s). One should always stay in prayer and faith

We must believe in living an eternal life with Christ, and how the apostle John advised us in scripture that, we need to focus more on Christ and the new life that will be provided to us once "this" life is over and done. That second we forget that Satan is the ruler of the earth that we trod on today, is when we adversely leave ourselves open and venerable to his destruction.

We must also remind ourselves that Satan does not love us the same way Christ loves us. As a matter of fact, Satan hates us with a passion. His desire is to destroy our faith in God.

Our society is full of those things that are more applicable to pleasing man, instead of pleasing our Father, who art in heaven. We often look to others (fleshly things) for answers, as opposed to seeking God for our answers. When we do this,(look to others for answers as opposed to God), we are often subjected to doing those things that are not pleasing to our Lord and Savior, which again, leaves doors open for the manipulation and destruction of our lives coming from Satan and his clever demons.

Angels do good work while Satan and his demons do whatever it takes for them to get our minds, hearts, and souls, to cross over into darkness, again – only because he(Satan) did not want to be second to God's creation(us).

Adam and Eve (God's creation) were very aware of the serpent (Satan), and wanted no parts of Satan after Satan tempted them to eat the forbidden fruit, and as a consequence lost grace with God.

The first book of Adam and Eve; in chapter twenty of Joseph Lumpkin's lost books of the Bible, quotes, "O God, take us away to some other place, where the serpent cannot come near us again and rise against us. For I fear that it might find your handmaid Eve alone and kill her, for its eyes are hideous and evil. But God said to Adam and Eve, "don't be afraid. From now on, I will not let it come near you. I have driven it away from you and this mountain. I will not leave in the ability to hurt you." Then Adam and Eve worshiped before God and gave him thanks and praised him for having delivered them from death." [98]

---

[98] Lumpkin, Joseph B. *Lost Books of the Bible: The Great Rejected Text*. {Joseph B. Lumpkin, 2009}, p. 21.

PART 4

CONTROVERSY: HELL - DOES IT EXIST?

---

*B*ecause of tensions with some of the Presidential election candidates today, there has been an increase in social media that say there is no heaven or hell. People believe that we are in the last days, and this is where Satan gets his diligence by confusing believers and non-believers.

I learned years ago, as an undergrad, never to get into heated conversations about scripture, especially if one of the parties refuse to consult scripture, as a base for debate. Maybe because he or she is a non-believer (atheist), which has happened before in the past as well.

God is very clear when he describes what goes on after death, and where an individual may end up, as a result of dishonoring grace and honoring the things that make Satan happy, as opposed to doing those things that make God happy.

Here I will take a moment to share some scripture that suggests that there is, in fact, a hell/hades.

I would like to begin with at least three important scriptures, which will convince a non-believer that there is a *place* where evil persons are tormented day and night because of their bad deeds during their lives.

"But the fearful, and *unbelieving,* and the abominable, and murderers, and whoremongers, and sorcerers, and idolaters, and all liars shall have their part in the lake which burneth with fire and brimstone: which is the second death." [99]

According to African Bible Commentary; in Revelation 21:3-5, God spoke with his people, stating that his creation of all things has been completed, and Revelation 21:8, suggests that all people that are wicked are to be barred from the kingdom of God. [100]

The next verse that I would like to suggest reading is Matthew 25:41, which says, "then shall he also say unto them on the left hand, Depart from me, ye cursed, into everlasting fire, prepared for the *devil* and his *angels.*"[101]

According to African Bible Commentary, Matthew 25:32-33, suggest that on one hand there will be righteous, and 25:41a,

---

[99] Felder, Cain Hope. *The Original African Heritage Study Bible* (King James Version). {Judson Press, 2007}, p. 1805.

[100] Adeyemo, Tokunboh. *Africa Bible Commentary: A One-Volume Commentary Written by 70 African Scholars.* World Alive Publishers, 2006, p. 1603.

[101] Felder, Cain Hope. *The Original African Heritage Study Bible* (King James Version). {Judson Press, 2007}, p. 1425.

Controversy: Hell - Does It Exist?

suggests that on the other hand will be those that are cursed. [102]

The last Scriptural verse that I would like to share that will explain to an unbeliever that hell does exist is Matthew 13:49-50. Matthew 13:49-50 says, "So shall it be at the end of the world: the angels shall come forth, and sever the wicked from among the just, and shall cast them into the furnace of fire; there shall be wailing and gnashing of teeth." [103]

The above scripture is self-explanatory, but according to the African Bible Commentary; suggests that God will sort the good from the bad, differentiating good people from the bad people. "The former will enter into his blessings and the latter into the *fiery furnace*."[104]

It is just important to share that John 8:44, is just as important because it says, (paraphrasing) that some are from their father – the devil, and that he was a sinner/murderer, from the beginning, and has no truth within him, and that he is a liar.

So, with that being said, we should be reminded that many people that do not believe that there is a place like a hell/fiery furnace, *should consult scripture* and not believe meme's circulating on social media as opposed to the scriptures.

---

[102] Adeyemo, Tokunboh. *Africa Bible Commentary: A One-Volume Commentary Written by 70 African Scholars*. World Alive Publishers, 2006, p. 1190.

[103] Felder, Cain Hope. *The Original African Heritage Study Bible* (King James Version). {Judson Press, 2007}, p. 1401.

[104] Adeyemo, Tokunboh. *Africa Bible Commentary: A One-Volume Commentary Written by 70 African Scholars*. World Alive Publishers, 2006, p. 1165.

Clinton Arnold[105] provides his analysis by adding that there are many evangelicals that are skeptical, regarding the existence of the powers of evil, and that there are many influences such as the media, secular education, as well as the press, and many other sources, that deny the existence of evil.

So, with that being said, if one does not believe in the existence of evil, then there are possibilities that one does not believe that there is a place called hell/hades, where the evil ones with being placed for the remainder of their existence after death here on earth.

Beilby and Eddy's [106] book, suggests that "Nothing commends Satan to the modern mind. It is bad enough that Satan is a spirit when our worldview has banned spirit from discourse and belief. But worse, he is evil, and our culture resolutely refuses to believe in the real existence of evil, preferring to regard it as a matter of systems break down that can be fixed with enough tinkering."

Perhaps Beilby and Eddy's comments are suggesting the same analysis as Clinton Arnold, that there are those that do not believe that Satan exist, so therefore, it is quite evident that they do not believe that there is a place that we refer to as hell.

---

[105] Arnold, Clinton E. *Powers of Darkness - Principalities & Powers in Paul's Letters* {Intervarsity Press, 1992}, p. 210.

[106] Beilby, James K. & Eddy, Paul Rhodes. *Understanding Spiritual Warfare.* {Baker Academic, 2012}, p. 47.

I will argue that Satan is a spirit, but in that same context, God is a spirit as well. God does well for humanity, and the Satan does whatever is corrupt to destroy humanity.

God is the creator of Satan, and being as though Satan is evil, along with other humans that he has tempted and won over their lives with corruption.

God is saying through his scripture, that there is a place where all the wretched people go, being in torment forever, is the written word of God, and therefore, God's words are true.

The torment that bad humans bring forth to other humans, hell is considered the place where the corrupt can be in harmony with their peers.

Conclusion

Many of social media have stated that they do not believe that there is a heaven or hell because they are suggesting that Jesus said, that heaven is within us and while heaven is within us, as Jesus stated in Luke 17:22, heaven and hell certainly does exist.

Various scripture(s) such as Revelation 21:3-5, Matthew 25:41, and Matthew 13;49-50, suggests that there is a hell and that hell is described as a place where bad people are sent and to suffer torment forever.

In closing; consulting scripture for advice and or information on how to live a decent life can be readily available by searching, and reading scripture, and finding the appropriate scripture, regarding what God, has to say about current situations, according to scripture, I am finding that hell does exist.

While there are those such as Clinton Arnold and Beilby and Eddy that suggest that there are people that exist, that do not believe in the existence of evil, one will argue that Scripture, definitely paints a totally different picture.

SATAN'S EVIL INTENTIONS?

Many earthly and destructive things that happen in life are the results of natural disasters. The results were not pleasing. Some say that natural disasters happen because God is not pleased, and, allows Satan to destroy the earth.

Spiritual beings like human beings have a mind of their own. They may choose to work for God or against God. However, the most dominant and disobedient were named Satan. [107]

Taking a look back at the book of Job: "This Satan questions God conviction that Job is serving God out of pure heart. Rather, he suggests that Job reveres God because of all the fringe benefits (1:9-11 2:4).

In response, God allows the Satan to test Job by destroying everything he possesses, including his children and his health (1:12-22; 2:4). This sets the stage for the epic poem that follows." [108]

---

[107] Boyd, Gregory A. *God at War – The Bible & Spiritual Conflict*. {IVP Academic, 1997}, p. 143.

[108] Boyd, Gregory A. *God at War – The Bible & Spiritual Conflict*. {IVP Academic, 1997}, p. 144

Hurricane Katrina was an example of this type of theory. One may question that God, Satan, caused a hurricane, Katrina. Natural causes are things such as tornadoes, hurricanes, earthquakes, or other natural causes. Many people seem to think that natural disasters are from the works of Satan and his demons, or that God allows these disasters to occur. According to Gavin Ortlund, many Christian circles, believe that because of the sins of Adam and Eve, are the results of natural disasters, such as hurricanes, tornadoes, etc. Ortlund suggests, that even though the world has these types of natural disasters, we can still live in a world that has a very loving God.[109]

After every tragedy, one can always expect God to show up with a blessing or learning experience.

For instance, yesterday, it was news that a young man stole a pair of Michael Jordon tennis shoes from a store, located in Brooklyn New York, and the young adult man began running with the box of shoes under his arm. The employee of the store took chase in his SUV. As a result, the driver of the SUV ran the young man over, and the young man's arm was cut off from his elbow and snapped off his arm, and was laying on the ground in the street.

Many have suggested that this was karma, because he stole from the store, God punished him by cutting off his arm.

---

[109] Ortlund, Gavin. "*On the Fall of Angels and the Fallenness of Nature: An Evangelical Hypothesis Regarding Natural Evil.*" Evangelical Quarterly 87, no. 2 (April 2015): 114-136. Academic Search Premier, EBSCOhost

Satan's Evil Intentions?

We cannot forget that Sodom and Gomora was destroyed by God because they were committing homosexual acts, and God was furious and destroyed the city. God destroyed the world because of sin and repopulated by Noah and his son's and wives.

Gabriel Fackre[110] suggests that the Biblical angels bring about good news as well as bad news, and in the case of Sodom and Gomora. The angels brought bad news regarding destroying the city, but good news for Lot regarding leaving before God destroyed the city of Sodom and Gomora

So, it's not so much of the evil intentions that God destroyed the earth, sin was the major cause that perhaps this was influenced by the temptation of Satan, which caused people to sin and behave in an inappropriate manner. This type of havoc has caused God to destroy a city and repopulated the earth. God says that vengeance is mines (Romans 12:19).

"While the angels do belong to the fore in doctrinal explorations of scripture's landscape, the demons must also be given their due. Creations "lower cosmos" can describe not our plane (contra Barth) but a depth dimension of powers and principalities (contra Tillich) that have set their face against the divine purposes." [111]

---

[110] Fackre, Gabriel. *"Angels heard and demons seen."* Theology Today 51, no. 3 (October 1994): 345. Academic Search Premier, EBSCOhost, p. 350.

[111] Fackre, Gabriel. *"Angels heard and demons seen."* Theology Today 51, no. 3 (October 1994): 345. Academic Search Premier, EBSCOhost, p. 348. Gabriel suggests, that the prophetic works of angels in scripture converts the Christian away from using, I. me or mines.

Exegetical Study of Angels & Demons

It becomes more evident that Satan's intentions were "good" when he was created. He was the angel of light, and the head angel of the cherubim angels, however, his intentions changed to evil intentions, before and after he was kicked out of heaven.

Lewis Sperry Chafer, [112] explains that "Scripture distinctly states that it was self – esteem, or pride, which incited this greatness of all angels to launch out upon an independent course of action (Ezek. 28:17; 1 Tim. 3:6). Satan does not lose faith in his enterprise until that future time when he is cast out of heaven. Of Satan at that time, it is written, "Woe to the inhabiters of the earth and the sea! For the devil is come down unto you, having great wrath, because he knows that he hath but a short time" (Rev 12; 12).

After reading the paragraph above, one wonders why anyone would choose evil over righteousness.

Before I turned my life over to Christ, I never picked up a Bible and read it for myself, and never understood scripture, even though I was raised in a popular Christian church, going to private school, and studied religion in school for one hour each day.

One must also remember, that angels can take on human forms. In some instances, one may have heard stories from many that say, that they were saved miraculously by an angel, and some perhaps were obviously tempted by bad angels.

---

[112] Chafer, Lewis Sperry. "*Angelology*." Bibliotheca Sacra 99, no. 396 (October 1942): 391-417. ATLA Religion Database with ATLASerials, EBSCOhost, p.394.

Satan's Evil Intentions?

We have noted earlier in this paper that angels do appear in human form, as the case with the title above in this paper, "Story of an angel."

Eric F.F. Bishop suggests, "Theology is enabled by the scripture to inform us that not only are there such spirits but a vast multitude of them: that they were made by God and Christ, and are immoral, and propagate not their species; and that these spirits have their chief residence in heaven, and enjoy the vision of God, whom they constantly praise, and punctually obey, without having sinned against him: that also, good angels are very intelligent beings, and of so great power, that one of them was able in a night to destroy a vast army: that they have degrees among themselves, are enemies to the devils, and fight against them that they can assume bodies like ours, and yet disappear in a trice." [113]

One has to be concerned whether bad angels can appear to cause strife and temp us to do the things that's against the word of God, and I will agree.

Bad angels work through people and often have them do and say things that can often annoy us and have us fight against them, however, our fight is not with them per-say, it is against the principalities of the evil one.

---

[113] Bishop, Eric Francis Fox. "*Angelology in Judaism, Islam and Christianity.*" Anglican Theological Review 46, no. 2 (April 1964): 142-154. ATLA Religion Database with ATLASerials, EBSCOhost, p. 143.

Eric Francis Bishop concludes by saying that a great portion of our society worships the enemies of mankind, and are the evil spirits that are not by nature.

The apostle Paul gives a brief explanation to the Corinthians to stay away from cults and their places, and you will not have to fear demons because they are not a problem.[114]

Considering that Satan may frequent in places of instability and confusion, such as bars, and nightclubs, one may want to stay away from places where Satan frequents as Paul states. That will decrease the chances of temptation and give Satan the influence to temp your mind with impure thoughts, thus giving Satan the fuel he needs, and the intent, to make you do those tings that corrupted.

Conclusion

The results of natural disasters are not pleasing to anyone that may have experienced them in the present, as well as in the past. Natural disasters are things such as hurricanes, tornadoes, earthquakes, and any other disaster from weather that may cause harm or even death.

We know in the past that God has destroyed the earth once when the angels were having sexual relations with female humans and producing offspring.

---

[114] Martin, Dale Basil. *"When Did Angels Become Demons?"* Journal of Biblical Literature 129, no. 4 (Winter2010 2010): 657-677. Academic Search Premier, EBSCO host, p. 674.

So, in our present situations that we are living in today, with the passing of laws that allow homosexuality, what's to say that God is not pleased with us, and have natural disasters occur as punishment?

As Gavin Ortlund suggests, that many Christian circles believe that because of the sins of Adam and Eve, are the results of natural disasters. On that note, God made a promise that he would never destroy the world as he had done before, regarding the flood, where only Noah and his three sons and their wives remained to repopulate the earth.

Consider the case of a young man in Brooklyn New York, that stole a pair of shoes, and, as a result, lost his arm when the owner of the store ran him over with his vehicle.

Can we agree that God or Satan was watching and allowed the young man to suffer because of his sin(stealing) and was not protected by his guardian angel?

Satan often tempts people and often people have evil intentions and commit crimes that deserve just punishment, but one has to ask him or herself, were these God's intentions, or did God allow Satan to do harm as the young man's punishment? After all, God tells us in Romans 12:19, that vengeance is mines.

We must, in any event, choose good over evil. Most case scenario, those that choose to do evil things, often pay with a heavy price. Those that remain faithful and choose to do good are often rewarded with an overflow of blessings.

Exegetical Study of Angels & Demons

Angels can take human form as we had read in scripture in the book of Genesis 19 when two angels arrived at Sodom and Gomora. Many angels have done good things, as well as Satan appearing to Jesus in the book of Matthew 4:1-11.

Also, Satan and his demons work through people. One might think that an argument that he or she is having with another person is with that person, but your argument is really with Satan and his demons. Arguments are considered pointless.

Be reminded that the cults, as well as places where Satan frequents, should be avoided. Nightclubs and bars often are full of rowdy people that drink alcohol in access. Nothing good comes from one that abuses alcohol or places where people get together and discuss cultic matters.

MENTAL ILLNESS

Do Satan and his demons have anything to do with mental illness?

I have spent a large portion of my life in law enforcement. The majority of my law enforcement career was spent working for the Federal Government at a mental hospital facility in Washington D.C., as a Federal Police Officer, and a Psychiatric Forensic Technician.

While working as a Psychiatric Forensic Technician, I spent quality time with patients on a one on one basis as a counselor/ nurse/ U.S. Marshall – all in one.

As a Psychiatric Forensic technician, I supervised 18 patients that were found by the courts to be "Not Guilty By Reasons of Insanity." The patients were housed on my ward, which was a minimum, maximum security ward. There were a few patients on my ward that worked part time jobs or let out on release but had to return to the ward at a certain hour.

I have had interactions with mass murderers, rapist, drug addicts, husbands and boyfriends that killed, or murdered their significant other, and literally ate them after killing them. You name it; they were on my ward.

However, the question comes to mind, what causes an individual to cross the lines into a severe mental status? Does Satan have anything to do with it? After all, he is a master, when it comes to manipulation.

Ron Phillips [115] suggests that mental illness is a very controversial topic in the Christian circles, and he feels that mental illness *is not the result of the demonic attack*, and I beg to differ, because of *my personal experiences* on the topic.

In cases where a person was normal, but he or she experimented with drugs, and as a result, they ended up killing one of their parents.

While I am writing this, I am thinking of a man in the back of my thought, and I wish not to disclose his name, but picturing his face while I'm typing. We would play pool together on the ward, but he was also a very dangerous man, and often had to be restrained and put into seclusion for a violent outburst because of severe schizophrenia. The doctors used electric shock therapy as a treatment that did not work.

---

[115] Phillips, Ron. *Demons & Spiritual Warfare*. {Charisma House, 2010}, p. 99.

Ron Phillips [116] suggests that when a mentally ill person is medicated with therapy, and therapy and medication do not work, is when there is a need for demonic operation. I do not agree. First, Mr. Phillips said that mental illness is not the result of the demonic attack but then changes by saying that when medication and therapy don't work, then perhaps the patient will require a demonic operation.

Many patients hear voices, and sometimes the voices can make them act out in violence. For instance, on Friday's, if the patients on my ward were good, staff would treat the to a Blockbuster movie and popcorn.

There was one patient in particular on some nights, he would hear voices, and as a result, knock the television on the floor and say, "My Aunt is inside the television." Obviously, he did not care too much for his aunt. His aunt, in his mind, his invisible aunt caused a lot of problems for staff, because he acted out when he believed that his aunt was near him.

Conclusion

We have asked the question whether or not Satan has anything to do with an individual being mentally ill, and we have determined that mental illness is a controversial topic.

---

[116] Phillips, Ron. *Demons & Spiritual Warfare*. {Charisma House, 2010},p. 99

However, I have come to a conclusion – from working inside a mental institution for the criminally insane that, when an individual experiments with drugs, he or she takes on the risk of hallucinating to the point where he or she becomes mentally ill or lose their minds completely and never regain normalcy.

Also, Ron Phillips seems to suggest that when a person does not respond to being treated by medication for mental illness, then perhaps there will be a need for demonic procedures.

HOMOSEXUALITY

Another problem that I see that is perhaps demonic is transexuals. First, let me be clear that I personally have no problems with the gay society. God wants us to love everyone, not just some. My problem with gays is their lifestyle that goes against the principles God set for us as a guide.

In the 1980's the American Psychological Association announced that homosexuality is a mental illness, and from my personal experiences dealing with mental patients, I can see how a homosexual acts out as a male or female – when they are the opposite sex of who they are trying to portray. The LGBT community confronted the APA to have their findings changed and considered it as discrimination.

I do believe that transsexuals or anyone that portrays to be other than the sex that he or she were genetically born as – suffers from a mental disorder, regardless if he or she *FEELS* that way.

Gurvinder Kalra[117] summarizes that human sexuality plays a chief role regarding an individual's existence as well as their functioning in life, and right of wrong sexuality defines a person's attitude that will ultimately affect social attitudes.

Bingham and Banner[118] examine the definition of mental disorder and suggests that the definition of mental disorder was the motivating factor by the declassification of homosexuality from the Diagnostic and Statistical Manual in 1973. They have argued that relying on scientific theory fails to agree with a strong definition of mental disorder that eliminates homosexuality.

One of the biggest lies in America today, is that a person is born gay. "The person often concludes that he or she must have been born as a genetically predetermined homosexual even though, as we have seen, *this conclusion is not supported by the findings of research.*" [119]

The question needs to be answered regarding whether there is any evil associated with homosexuality, regarding temptation from Satan and his demons.

I would propose that it is good and evil in the world we live in today.

---

[117] Kalra, Gurvinder, Antonio Ventriglio, and Dinesh Bhugra. 2015. "Sexuality and mental health: Issues and what next?." *International Review Of Psychiatry* 27, no. 5: 463-469. *Academic Search Premier*, EBSCO*host*

[118] Bingham, Rachel, and Natalie Banner. 2014. "The definition of mental disorder: evolving but dysfunctional?." *Journal Of Medical Ethics* 40, no. 8: 537-542. *Academic Search Premier*, EBSCO*host*.

[119] Collins, Gary R. *"Christian Counseling: A comprehensive guide"*. World publishing 1988,p. 285.

Homosexuality

I would also submit – that the act of pursuing a homosexual act, certainly does not come from the Lord, so, therefore, it must come from Satan. Again, as we know, that Satan seeks to destroy.

Gary Collins[120] agrees with my suggestion that homosexual feelings and tendencies, as well as desires, cannot be found in scripture, but when a person dwells on unpure thoughts and lust, then it becomes a sin. Collins suggests that the Christian can be tempted, just like Jesus was tempted.

I agree and advocate that *anyone regardless of his or her religious preference; their faith can and will be tested.*

"Scripture shows that we can avoid dwelling on lustful thoughts or giving in to *sinful temptations* of any kind, including homosexual temptations."[121]

"Paul believes in heavenly spirits, good, evil, or neutral, who exercise an influence

Over the salvation of men. He borrows his angelical categories mainly from two currents of thought and of expression which can call that of the "Angels" and that of the "Powers." [122] Satan is the

---

[120] Collins, Gary R. *"Christian Counseling: A comprehensive guide"*. World publishing 1988, p. 282.

[121] Collins, Gary R. *"Christian Counseling: A comprehensive guide"*. World publishing 1988, p.282

[122] Benoit, Pierre. 1983. *"Pauline angelology and demonology: reflexions on designations of heavenly powers and on the origin of angelic evil according to Paul."* Religious Studies Bulletin 3, no. 1: 1-18. ATLA Religion Database with ATLASerials, EBSCOhost, p. 1&3

most frequent in regards o Pauline corpus – which Paul calls evil spirits. According to Benoit.

So, one must wonder if evil spirits are behind the influence of deceiving people to think they are one sex when they are the opposite sex of their birth. I would suggest two different answers.

1. The person is conceived and tricked by evil demonic spirits into believing that they are female when they were born male and visa-verse.
2. The lack of parental guidance of one particular sex in the family. For example, a male may act like a woman if there is no male presence in the household.

Gary Collins suggests the following: Children in the same family do not become homosexual though there may be comparable parent-child interactions.

However, Collins suggest homosexuality has been found when:

1. "Mothers distrust or fear women and teach this to their sons
2. Mothers distrust or fear men and teach this to their daughters
3. A son is surrounded by too many females(Mothers, sisters, aunts) but he has limited contact with adult males. Thus he learns to think and act like a girl
4. Parents who wanted a daughter but instead have a son subtly raise the boy to think and act like a girl(a similar situation arises when parents wanted a son but instead have

a daughter); in both cases, the child has great confusion about sexual identity and orientation." [123]

Conclusion

The question war raised in regards to whether Satan and his demons are one of the reasons why men or women commit homosexuality. My conclusion is that Satan is a manipulator and can persuade people to believe that homosexuality is fine, but scripture tells us that this is false.

Also, we have noted that there is no research that supports that a person is born gay.

The American Psychological Association had once researched that homosexuality is a mental illness, however, as time progressed, the LGBT community had that research and analysis changed, and considered the finding as a form of discrimination.

Noted that, Gary Collins suggests that homosexual feelings and tendencies and desires cannot be found in scripture, but their thoughts that they may have on those desires becomes a sin, and in some cases can be avoided if one would be selective of places where sin is prevalent.

Transexual behaviors can be attributed to the manipulation of Satan and his demons, and thus, can be categorized as a mental illness from people that are observing this strange behavior.

---

[123] Collins, Gary R. *"Christian Counseling: A comprehensive guide"*. World Publishing 1988, p.283.

Gary Collins has noted various reasons that should not be ignored regarding why a child may begin having homosexual tendencies.

BRIEF ANALYSIS OF THE ENEMY

There is a real war going on with the enemy. The enemy is Satan and his demons. [124] Revelation 12:9, advises us that "The great dragon was cast out, that ancient serpent called the Devil and Satan, who deceives the whole world."

If we are not careful, and if we are not relying on Christ to save us from the eternal damnation, we can easily be misled and deceived by Satan and his demons.

John 3:16-18 says, "For God so loved the world, that he gave his only begotten Son, that whosoever believeth in him should not perish, but have everlasting life." [125]

According to the Africa Bible Commentary, "The process of the new birth began in heaven when God's love for humankind

---

[124] Phillips, Ron. *Angels and Demons*. {Lake Mary, Florida: Charisma House, 2015}, p.124.

[125] Felder, Cain Hope. *The Original African Heritage Study Bible* (King James Version). {Judson Press, 2007}, p. 1535.

led him to send his only Son, Jesus Christ, into the world to die for the world." [126]

Satan knows that his existence here on earth is limited, so his agenda is to include you and me when his time has ended to eternal damnation.

"They are exiled to earth and are permitted to temp people. When Elohim's (God the Father) purpose has been fulfilled, Lucifer and his demons will be exiled to the "Outer Darkness," completely cut off from divine light and love." [127]

In the nineteenth century, there was a Frenchman named, Leo Taxil, who excelled in occult hoaxes, perpetrated that Freemasonry was related to Lucifer.[128]

Let me be the first to assure you that Prince Hall Freemasonry has nothing to do with Lucifer. The "Prince Hall" Freemasons are an organization of a men's fraternity; that does good work for the betterment of the community as well as for the betterment of the masons, making them better men for their families and their communities.

---

[126] Adeyemo, Tokunboh. *Africa Bible Commentary: A One-Volume Commentary Written by 70 African Scholars.* World Alive Publishers, 2006, p. 1285.

[127] Guiley, Rosemary Ellen. *The Encyclopedia of Demons and Demonology.* {Checkmark Books, 2009}, p. 134.

[128] Guiley, Rosemary Ellen. *The Encyclopedia of Demons and Demonology.* {Checkmark Books, 2009}, p.134.

"Satan is the arch enemy of God, the opponent of all that is good; Satan does Evil." [129]

Conclusion

There is no research that supports the theory that a person is born gay.

Also, the American Psychological Association has stated that they believe that homosexuality is a mental illness.

As time took its course, the LGBT community had the results from the American Psychological Association reversed.

While homosexual feelings and desires cannot be found in scripture, a homosexuals thoughts, and desires, thus becomes a sin.

If one's thoughts are aggressive enough to be a sin, then it's common to suggest that homosexual activity includes transsexual activity on any level becomes a sin and becomes the desires of Satan.

---

[129] Stokes, Ryan E. "Satan, Yhwh's Executioner." *Journal Of Biblical Literature* 133, no. 2 (Summer2014 2014): 251-270. *Academic Search Premier*, EBSCO*host*, p. 251

CLOSING REMARKS

"The Christian worldview summons people to follow Christ, to recognize and obey the truth that sets them free. To the Jews who had believed him, Jesus said, If you hold to my teaching, you are my disciples. Then you will know the truth will set you free" (John 8:31-32). [130]

Many today as I have noted earlier, either do not believe in Christ and believe he never existed and that Christ was made up by the early Christian church. From this, I can add by saying that believers I have come across, have a noticeable presence glow about their person. Many are successful in their time, with the gifts and blessings that come from above.

Those that are having trouble in his or her lives, I have noticed are living life on their terms and have no time for anything that has to do with living the life as Christ has showed for us, as an example.

---

[130] Groothuis, Douglas. "Christian Apologetics" IVP Academic, 2011, p.93-94.

Satan is always seeking to devour any relationship that we are trying to have with God. Satan will often as I have stated earlier, will work through people.

> A perfect example is a family. Family can be some of the most cut-throat to the core and sometimes vile persons. The family runs deep to the core of one's heart. Satan can impact one's life by using family members as his tools for weapons. I have seen this happen time and time again. The best course is to stay clear of drama and confusion from friends as well as family members when they become nasty and vile, then Satan has no tools to use against you.

Elaine Pagels [131] suggests that the New Testament gospels place Jesus in the context of a cosmic war with evil. God acts through Jesus to encounter evil forces that are prevailing in our present world attacking.[132]

In Revelation 20, God talks about releasing Satan after one thousand years, and Gary Harris has a reason for Satan's release.

---

[131] Pagels, Elaine. "The social history of Satan, Part II." *Journal of The American Academy Of Religion* 62, no. 1 (Spring94 1994): 17. *MasterFILE Premier*, EBSCO*host, p. 17.*

[132] Pagels, Elaine. "The social history of Satan, Part II." *Journal of The American Academy Of Religion* 62, no. 1 (Spring94 1994): 17. *MasterFILE Premier*, EBSCO*host,p. 17.*

Closing Remarks

"Satan must be released so that God can demonstrate to Israel and the world the veracity of his covenant promises, completely and precisely fulfilling them in a minute and specific details – all the way to the arrival to the eternal state." [133]

God will fulfill his promises and defeat Satan in the most mighty way one can attest. Satan has caused so much stress and many strange behaviors. (Satan and his demons) enjoy destroying human beings with his entire evil empire of hostile spirits. [134]

Ignore Satan and pray and trust in God (All the Time). Trust in God and live life according to his law and accept nothing different. Enjoy Life and be kind and humble to everyone. Your angels are always watching out for you… trust them and the Lord and ignore Satan's temptation. God loves you and so do I.

Peace and Many Blessings!
David Vincent Williams

---

[133] Harris, Greg (Gregory H). "Must Satan be released?: indeed he must be: toward a biblical understanding of Revelation 20:3." *The Master's Seminary Journal* 25, no. 1 (2014 2014): 11-27. *ATLA Religion Database with ATLASerials*, EBSCO*host, p. 11*.

[134] Pagels, Elaine H. "The social history of Satan, the 'intimate enemy': a preliminary sketch." *Harvard Theological Review* 84, no. 2 (April 1991): 105-128. *ATLA Religion Database with ATLASerials*, EBSCO*host*.

BIBLIOGRAPHY

Adeyemo, Tokunboh. *Africa Bible Commentary: A One-Volume Commentary Written by 70 African Scholars*. World Alive Publishers, 2006.

Angelology." Merriam-Webster.com. Accessed September 30, 2015. http://www.merriam-webster.com/dictionary/angelology.

Agamben, Giorgio. "*ANGELS*." Angelaki: Journal of the Theoretical Humanities 16, no. 3 (September 2011): 117-123. Academic Search Premier, EBSCOhost (accessed September 10, 2015).

Albright, William Foxwell. "*What were the cherubim?.*" Biblical Archaeologist 1, no. 1 (February 1938): 1-3. ATLA Religion Database with ATLASerials, EBSCOhost (accessed September 12, 2015).

Areopagite, Pseudo – Dionysius. The *Celestial Hierarchy*. {Limovia.net, 2013}.

Arnold, Clinton E. *Powers of Darkness - Principalities & Powers in Paul's Letters* {Intervarsity Press, 1992}.

Arnold, Johann Christoph. "*Exploring Heaven & HELL.*" USA Today Magazine 131, no. 2692 (January 2003): 58. Academic Search Premier, EBSCOhost (accessed September 28, 2015).

Bayer, Oswald. "Angels Are Interpreters." *Lutheran Quarterly* 13, no. 3 (1999 1999): 271-284. *ATLA Religion Database with ATLASerials*, EBSCO*host* (accessed October 23, 2015).

Beilby, James K. & Eddy, Paul Rhodes. *Understanding Spiritual Warfare*. {Baker Academic, 2012}.

Benoit, Pierre. 1983. "*Pauline angelology and demonology: reflexions on designations of heavenly powers and on the origin of angelic evil according to Paul.*" Religious Studies Bulletin 3, no. 1: 1-18. ATLA Religion Database with ATLASerials, EBSCOhost (accessed September 28, 2015).

Bethany House Publishers. *Everything the Bible says about Angels and Demons*. {Bloomington Minnesota: Bethany House Publishers, 2012}.

Bingham, Rachel, and Natalie Banner. 2014. "*The definition of mental disorder: evolving but dysfunctional?.*" *Journal Of Medical Ethics* 40, no. 8: 537-542. *Academic Search Premier*, EBSCO*host* (accessed February 24, 2016).

Bishop, Eric Francis Fox. *"Angelology in Judaism, Islam, and Christianity."* Anglican Theological Review 46, no. 2 (April 1964): 142-154. ATLA Religion Database with ATLASerials, EBSCOhost (accessed September 10, 2015).

Boa, Kenneth D & Bowman, Robert M Jr. *"Sense & Nonsense about Angels & Demons"*. {Zondervan, 2007}.

Boyd, Gregory A. *God at War – "The Bible & Spiritual Conflict"*. {IVP Academic, 1997}.

Camille, Alice. *"Where have all the demons gone?."* U.S. Catholic 68, no. 2 (February 2003): 45. Academic Search Premier, EBSCOhost (accessed September 28, 2015).

Chafer, Lewis Sperry. *"Angelology."* Bibliotheca Sacra 99, no. 396 (October 1942): 391-417. ATLA Religion Database with ATLASerials, EBSCOhost (accessed September 10, 2015).

Collins, Gary R. *"Christian Counseling: A comprehensive guide"*. World Publishing 1988.

Davidson, Gustav. *"A Dictionary of Angels including the fallen angels."* {The Free Press, 1967}.

"Demonology." Merriam-Webster.com. Accessed September 30, 2015. http://www.merriam-webster.com/dictionary/demonology

Dickason, C. Fred. *Angels – Elect &Evil*. {Moody Publishers, 1975}.

Draper, Scott, and Joseph O. Baker. "*Angelic Belief as American Folk Religion.*" *Sociological Forum* 26, no. 3 (September 2011): 623-643. *Academic Search Premier*, EBSCO*host* (accessed October 6, 2015).

Elwell, Walter A. *Evangelical Dictionary of Theology*. Baker Academic, 2001.

Ellwood, Robert S. "*Lure of the Sinister: the unnatural history of Satanism.*" *Nova Religio* 8, no. 1 (July 2004): 114-115. *ATLA Religion Database with ATLASerials*, EBSCO*host* (accessed November 19, 2015).

Fackre, Gabriel. "*Angels heard and demons seen.*" Theology Today 51, no. 3 (October 1994): 345. Academic Search Premier, EBSCOhost (accessed September 28, 2015).

Felder, Cain Hope. *The Original African Heritage Study Bible* (King James Version). {Judson Press, 2007}.

Felder, Cain Hope. *True to our Native Land*. Fortress Press, 2007.

Garrett, Susan R. 2009. "*Jesus and the angels.*" Word & World 29, no. 2: 162-169. *ATLA Religion Database with ATLASerials*, EBSCO*host* (accessed October 23, 2015).

Garrett, Susan R. *"The Origin of Satan: the New Testament origins of Christianity's demonization of Jews, pagans, and heretics."* Journal Of Biblical Literature 116, no. 1 (1997 1997): 134-136. *ATLA Religion Database with ATLASerials*, EBSCO*host* (accessed November 17, 2015).

Gibbs, Nancy, and Sam Allis. *"Angels among us. (cover story)."* Time 142, no. 27 (December 27, 1993): 56. *MAS Ultra - School Edition*, EBSCO*host* (accessed October 23, 2015).

Giulea, Dragoş-Andrei. *"The Watchers' Whispers: Athenagoras's Legatio 25,1-3 and the Book of the Watchers."* Vigiliae Christianae 61, no. 3 (August 2007): 258-281. *Academic Search Premier*, EBSCO*host* (accessed October 23, 2015).

Groothuis, Douglas. *"Christian Ap*ologetics" IVP Academic, 2011.

Guiley, Rosemary Ellen. *The Encyclopedia of Demons and Demonology*. {Checkmark Books, 2009}.

Harris, Greg (Gregory H). *"Must Satan be released?: indeed, he must be: toward a biblical understanding of Revelation 20:3."* The Master's Seminary Journal 25, no. 1 (2014 2014): 11-27. *ATLA Religion Database with ATLASerials*, EBSCO*host* (accessed February 27, 2016).

Hammenstede, Albert. 1945. "*The holy angels and we.*" *Orate Fratres* 19, no. 9: 400-406. *ATLA Religion Database with ATLASerials*, EBSCO*host* (accessed October 23, 2015).

Hozid, Zachary. "Gender Identity "Disorder"? *A Critique of the Binary Approach to Gender.*" *Ethical Human Psychology & Psychiatry* 15, no. 2 (July 2013): 135-138. *Academic Search Premier*, EBSCO*host* (accessed February 24, 2016).

Jensen, Lene Arnett. "*Conceptions of God and the Devil Across the Lifespan: A Cultural-Developmental Study of Religious Liberals and Conservatives.*" *Journal For The Scientific Study Of Religion* 48, no. 1 (March 2009): 121-145. *Academic Search Premier*, EBSCO*host* (accessed November 17, 2015).

Kalra, Gurvinder, Antonio Ventriglio, and Dinesh Bhugra. 2015. "*Sexuality and mental health: Issues and what next?.*" *International Review Of Psychiatry* 27, no. 5: 463-469. *Academic Search Premier*, EBSCO*host* (accessed February 24, 2016).

Kent, Paul. "*Knowing your Bible.*" Barbour Publishing 2013.

Kreeft, Peter. *Angels and Demons, What do we really know about them?* {San Francisco: Ignatius Press, 1995}.

Landes, George M. "*Shall we neglect the angels.*" *Union Seminary Quarterly Review* 14, no. 4 (May 1959): 19-25. *ATLA Religion Database with ATLASerials*, EBSCO*host* (accessed October 23, 2015).

Lumpkin, Joseph. *The Apocrypha: Including Books from the Bible*. {Joseph Lumpkin, 2009}.

Lumpkin, Joseph B. *Lost Books of the Bible: The Great Rejected Text*. {Joseph B. Lumpkin, 2009}.

Martin, Dale Basil. "*When Did Angels Become Demons?*" Journal of Biblical Literature 129, no. 4 (Winter2010 2010): 657-677. Academic Search Premier, EBSCOhost (accessed September 10, 2015).

McDowell, Josh & Stewart, Don. *Answers to tough questions*. Tyndale House Publishers, 1986.

McLeod, Frank E. *Angels Q&A*. {Frank E. McLeod, 2013}.

Medway, Gareth J. *Lure of the Sinister: The Unnatural History of Satanism*. University Press, 2001.

Moreland, J.P. www.jp.moreland.com accessed on January 25, 2016.

Moshier, David. *Satan is no Angel (and never was)*. {David Moshier, 2013}.

Moshier, David. *The Satan Series*. {David Moshier, 2013}.

NIV Study Bible. Zondervan, 1973.

Oldridge, Darren. *The Devil – A Very Short Introduction.* {Oxford University Press, 2012}.

Ortlund, Gavin. "*On the Fall of Angels and the Fallenness of Nature: An Evangelical Hypothesis Regarding Natural Evil.*" Evangelical Quarterly 87, no. 2 (April 2015): 114-136. Academic Search Premier, EBSCOhost (accessed September 12, 2015).

Osborn, Lawrence. "Entertaining Angels: *Their Place in Contemporary* Theology." *Tyndale Bulletin* 45, no. 2 (November 1994): 273-296. *ATLA Religion Database with ATLASerials*, EBSCO*host* (accessed October 23, 2015).

Pagels, Elaine H. "*The social history of Satan, the 'intimate enemy': a preliminary sketch.*" Harvard Theological Review 84, no. 2 (April 1991): 105-128. *ATLA Religion Database with ATLASerials*, EBSCO*host* (accessed February 27, 2016).

Pagels, Elaine. "*The social history of Satan, Part II.*" Journal *Of The American Academy Of Religion* 62, no. 1 (Spring94 1994): 17. *MasterFILE Premier*, EBSCO*host* (accessed February 27, 2016).

Peterson, Erik. 1938. "*From other lands: the holy angels.*" *Orate Fratres* 12, no. 5: 212-218. *ATLA Religion Database with ATLASerials*, EBSCO*host* (accessed October 23, 2015).

Phillips, Ron. *Angels and Demons.* {Lake Mary, Florida: Charisma House, 2015}.

Phillips, Ron. *Demons & Spiritual Warfare*. {Charisma House, 2010}.

Phillips, Ron. *Our Invisible Allies*. {Lake Mary, Florida: Charisma House, 2009}.

Reichert, Jenny, and James T Richardson. "*Decline of a moral panic: a social psychological and socio-legal examination of the current status of Satanism.*" *Nova Religio* 16, no. 2 (November 2012): 47-63. *ATLA Religion Database with ATLASerials*, EBSCO*host* (accessed November 17, 2015).

Russell, Jeffrey Burton. "Getting Satan Behind Us." *First Things* 57, (November 1995): 40-45. *ATLA Religion Database with ATLASerials*, EBSCO*host* (accessed November 17, 2015).

Skolnick, Irving H. "*THE HIDDEN MISSION OF BIBLICAL ANGELS.*" Jewish Bible Quarterly 38, no. 1 (January 2010): 21-31. Academic Search Premier, EBSCOhost (accessed September 12, 2015).

Steimle, Edmund Augustus. 1969. "*Children and angels.*" Union Seminary Quarterly Review 24, no. 3: 265-271. *ATLA Religion Database with ATLASerials*, EBSCO*host* (accessed October 23, 2015).

Stokes, Ryan E. "Satan, Yhwh's Executioner." *Journal Of Biblical Literature* 133, no. 2 (Summer2014 2014): 251-270.

Academic Search Premier, EBSCO*host* (accessed February 27, 2016).

Tremmel, William C. "*Satan - the dark side.*" *Iliff Review* 42, no. 1 (1985 1985): 3-12. *ATLA Religion Database with ATLASerials*, EBSCO*host* (accessed November 17, 2015).

Unger, Merrill F. *Biblical Demonology – A Study of Spiritual Forces at Work Today.* {Kregel Publications, 1994}.

Welker, Michael. "*Angels in the biblical traditions.*" Theology Today 51, no. 3 (October 1994): 367. Academic Search Premier, EBSCOhost (accessed September 12, 2015).

Whiston, Williams & Stebbing, H. *The Life and Works of Flavius Josephus*. The John Winston Company.

Wilken, Robert L. "*With angels and archangels.*" Pro Ecclesia 10, no. 4 (September 2001): 460-474. *ATLA Religion Database with ATLASerials*, EBSCO*host* (accessed October 23, 2015).

Windsor, Rudolph R. "*From Babylon to Timbuktu*" Windsor Golden Series, 2003.

Woodward, Kenneth L., and Anne Underwood. "*Angels.*" *Newsweek* 122, no. 26 (December 27, 1993): 52. *Academic Search Premier*, EBSCO*host* (accessed October 23, 2015).